MW01591659

# Wake Me When It's Over:

### From the Board Room to the Twilight Zone and the Faithfulness of God

*by*

## Linda Rios Brook

Lisa -
my beloved co-laborer
in the Kingdom -

**AmErica House**
**Baltimore**

First printing

ISBN: 1-58851-291-6
PUBLISHED BY AMERICA HOUSE BOOK PUBLISHERS
www.publishamerica.com
Baltimore

Printed in the United States of America

# Dedication

This book is lovingly dedicated to
Dr. Barbara Leonard Schulz,
without whose insistence, perseverance,
encouragement and patience,
it would never have been written.

# Acknowledgments

I would like to express my heartfelt thanks to several individuals who influenced the writing of this book:

To my husband Larry Brook who never lost faith in me.

To the Lakeland Foundation Board for their continual support: Norman Hagfors, Pastor Alan Langstaff, Jerry Peltier, Rich Runbeck, and Pastor Morris Vaagenes.

To all the investors of KLGT who caught the vision.

To all the employees of KLGT WB 23 from the purchase and sale of the station, whose tireless efforts made a miracle.

# Endorsement

"In <u>Wake Me When It's Over</u>, Linda Rios Brook, one of the Midwest's highly regarded power brokers, tells her story of faith in the marketplace. The story is well told and will grip you, as it should. All who want to impact the marketplace for Christ should read this book."

Rich Marshall
Author, <u>God @ Work</u>

# Contents

# FOREWORD

Is it possible that the kingdom of God extends beyond the four walls of our churches?

How might we expect God to answer our prayer: "Thy kingdom come, Thy will be done on earth as it is in heaven?"

These are simple questions, but they are not trivial. Understanding the issues raised by these questions could tip the scales toward seeing fundamental changes for the better come to our communities. This book will open your eyes to a crucial component for actually introducing tangible signs of God's kingdom throughout the warp and woof of our cities. Some of us have been calling this powerful activity of God "marketplace ministries."

Most of us are quite familiar with how Christian believers minister in churches or in parachurch organizations. But when believers are out in the workplace, which they are most of the time, can their activities there be seen as equally legitimate "ministry?" Linda Rios Brook thinks so, and no one I know has described in more eloquent prose how a servant of God can faithfully role model divinely-ordained ministry in the marketplace throughout a fascinating career.

One of the reasons why I love this book is that Linda has written it in such an unreligious way. As I was reading, it occurred to me that I don't believe that I am acquainted with a single pastor or other professional Christian leader who could say things about life out there in the marketplace with the freshness and frankness and vitality and authenticity that Linda scatters throughout every page. Moments after I began to read <u>Wake Me When It's Over</u> I was hooked, and you will be also. It is very difficult to put this book down, and it is even more difficult to get Linda's vibrant experiences with life out of your mind when you are finished.

The strategic role of marketplace ministries as an avenue for God's kingdom to come to earth as it is in heaven is destined, in my judgment, to become one of the hottest and highest profile topics in the whole Christian world during this first decade of the 2000s. As this book begins to spread its message through the body of Christ, we still find ourselves in the phase of asking questions, forging definitions, and building understanding between leaders of the *nuclear* church and leaders of the *extended* church, out there in the real world.

It is not a new thought to affirm that God has put His people in the marketplace as salt and light. But the frustrating fact is that, through recent years, the overall influence of believers on society in general has been minimal. Many would agree that over the last generation or two the moral and spiritual fabric of American society has gone downhill. In many ways America looks less like heaven now than it did fifty years ago. But I am convinced that this is going to change and change radically.

It will be an army of believers like Linda Rios Brook that makes this happen. God will use leaders like Linda to catalyze marketplace ministers, to help pastors learn how to empower them, to show that ministry in the boardroom is a divine equivalent to ministry in the Sunday School class, and to open strategic doors for the expansion of God's kingdom on new levels.

When you read this book you will see what I mean!

C. Peter Wagner, Chancellor

Wagner Leadership Institute
Box 63060
Colorado Springs CO 80962

# A Reader's Advisory

I had to finish writing this book before I understood why I wrote it. I have recently attended many seminars urging marketplace Christians to see their workplace as an opportunity for mission and evangelism. I have heard presenters assure business people that the Lord will reward them for seeing their work as their ministry I don't disagree with that at all. In fact, I am convinced that this view is a good one. However, in all seminars that I have attended, I have not heard one presenter tell the participants that when they take seriously the idea that their workplace is their ministry that all hell wakes up and takes notice. We encourage people to do something bold without telling them what will happen when they do. Yes, there are blessings, but marketplace ministry often triggers a spiritual attack against the person that he did not see coming and for which there are real consequences. This is what this book is about.

This is not a book about victimization. I lament the victim mentality that permeates so much of modern culture. I care deeply about and even cry for people who suffer devastating personal loss. I care about and even marvel at those who mourn their loss, deal with the travesty, and still manage to go on, often making the world a significantly better place.

Yes, there are legitimate cases and concerns of injustice and discrimination that Title VII is in place to address. But every business owner knows that there is also a litigious lunatic fringe in America that has spawned the perpetual-victim-society of the marketplace. Likewise, it is not uncommon for Christians themselves to develop a similar persecution complex and call it spiritual attack. It is rarely real discrimination and almost never spiritual attack. Business owners are very aware of the consequences of marketplace discrimination and most Christians live lives that are of very little interest to spiritual forces.

Discrimination is not the same thing as *offence*. We are not guaranteed in the constitution that we will never be offended. The New Testament positively guarantees that followers of Jesus will be *offended* and, unfortunately, *offensive*. Offence in some form happens to everyone. Short shrift happens to everyone. Bad timing happens to everyone. Disappointment comes to everyone. It is trite, but it is also true, that it isn't what happens to you so much as what you do with what happens to you. Bad things happen to the just and the unjust. Terrible and unfair things happen to people who do not deserve what has happened to them. This is a fallen world and in a fallen world, sometimes life stinks.

People who have had really tough breaks, and who cried, but did not whine have often inspired me. I have admired the ones, paraphrasing Rudyard Kipling *"who watched the things they gave their lives to broken, and stooped and built them up with worn out tools."* When my turn on the rack came, I wanted to be like them. I hope that I succeeded. People who know about the reading habits of Americans have told me that if I want anyone to read this book, I must share the pain, exploit the bias against Christianity and make the reader cry. If that is true, this will not be a best seller. But, this is probably not a story for the masses anyway. It is a story for warlords, eagles, and kings. It is for people who are on their way to something big who have not yet come to the fork in the road that the map does not show. It is a true story and a navigational handbook for those whom God is going to invite on a great adventure. If you need to cry, buy a romance novel.

# Chapter One

## God is a Wild Ride

If it hadn't been for that exorcism episode at that little church in Apple Valley, most of this likely would never have happened. But, when that poor woman curled up in a ball on the floor with her eyes rolled back in her head like that, spewing out obscenities, what was I supposed to do? There was no way the class I was teaching could go on with her rolling around there like that. I will admit that I was naïve. Deliverance ministry is as old as the Bible, so I just naturally assumed that even conservative Minnesotans knew that demons and spirits sometimes manifest in a spiritually charged atmosphere. Surely everyone has uttered the cliché "speak of the devil and he appears." It is true, you know, as are most clichés. That is how they get to cliché status. When we teach on the demonic realm, the demonic realm shows up. It never crossed my mind that this was going to be such a big deal. I should have guessed that when several of the students went screaming out the door that perhaps the demons in Minnesota were not accustomed to being tossed out like that. Of course I knew that one does not attempt the deliverance of a manifesting demon by one's self. So I turned to a girl named Mary who was the leader of the class and told her that she would have to help me. I told her that I wanted her to cover me with prayer and to pray in tongues while I dealt with the demon. She said, "I'll try but can I tell you something? I've never actually prayed out loud before and I don't pray in tongues." At that moment the demonized woman began convulsing and throwing up on

Mary's shoe. I've never seen anyone drop to her knees and pray harder, louder, or faster than Mary did.

Except for the vomiting, it was really a very tame deliverance and it was all over in a few minutes. It hardly merited the other students knocking each other over in their rush to get out door. But, as a friend of mine had said in a similar instance, if I had come out of the kitchen stark naked and swinging a dead chicken, I could not have cleared the room any faster. It wasn't like exorcism was a regular part of my teaching curriculum. I knew how to do it because I had been one of those who had been trained at a rather well known 5-day conference on healing and deliverance, conducted by Francis and Judith McNutt in 1987 near Jacksonville, Fla. I studied this part of ministry for the same reason that a person studies CPR. One hopes never to be called upon to use it, but one had better be prepared in case one is. The difference between praying for someone's *healing* without training and praying for someone's *deliverance* without training is this. Anyone can pray for the sick, trained or not, without doing any damage. The sick person might not get well, but it is highly unlikely that he will get worse. Deliverance, however, is very different. A person who is not trained in deliverance as a ministry should not practice on anyone. Indeed, the victim can end up in worse condition.

That is why when I was asked to "fill in" for a deliverance teacher at a crisis center for training lay ministers in healing, of which deliverance is often a prerequisite to healing, I agreed to do it. Who could have guessed that making that decision would mark the first day of the rest of my life? If it hadn't been for my involvement that day in Apple Valley, I am convinced that *I* would have remained beneath the radar screen of the tabloid press and never have become famous. My regular teaching emphasis was on scripture and the historicity of the gospels. I taught the kinds of topics that make tabloid editors yawn and are of very little interest to the local paparazzi. But just mention a demon and you've got fodder for inquiring minds that want to know.

I never could figure out why these tabloid writers became so fascinated with my every move. Believe me, I was the most ordinary person around. Well, except for that casting out demons part. A middle aged, unremarkable woman like me doesn't usually cause such a feeding frenzy in the gossip columns. It must have been that exorcism thing. Oh, I suppose that it could also have been because, at that time, I had a job in the media.

*****

I was the President and General Manager of the NBC affiliate in Minneapolis. I was the first woman to hold this position. It was a job that held glamour, and power, and position, and wealth. It was a job that causes other people to think that you are important. It was a job that a person works a lifetime to get and will sell his soul to keep. It was a job I cherished. And, it is a job that I no longer have. This is the story of how I managed to move from rising star to corporately unemployable in one crucial decision. It occurs to me that if you are reading this book, you are probably a Christian. As such, it may be that you have in your mind an image of what a person in whose life the Lord does something extraordinary, must be like. Before I tell this story, I think it is important to tell you that I will probably not meet that expectation. While I was not a "worldly Christian," I was very much a Christian who lived in the very middle of "worldliness."

Lydia was a seller of purple cloth. This meant that she dealt with the worldly wealthy who could afford purple cloth. Without a doubt, the same religious establishment that Jesus abhorred would have disdained Lydia. She used her position and her wealth to help Paul and most likely began the church at Thyatira. But many would have considered her skill at moving in and among the pagan rich to be inconsistent with the prevailing religiosity. She was able to use her business skills to advance the kingdom in a significant way, but many would have questioned her motives.

While I have never sold any purple cloth, I have worn a lot of it with designer labels attached. I could afford purple cloth because I was a very successful businesswoman, who loved the Lord and as such sincerely tried to use my position and my wealth to advance the kingdom of God. I was successful in business because I could move in and among the worldly powerful with a good deal of skill. When I entered a conference room in the penthouse suite of the NBC building in New York, no one said, "Oh, my, a religious woman just entered the room." They thought instead, "someone who can afford purple cloth just entered the room." In that environment, purple cloth symbolized position and power. I tell you this in the beginning of this book because I know that there is often an expectation for what a Christian woman ought to be like and if you hold such an expectation, I fear that I may disappoint you greatly. For one thing, I still wear purple cloth. I have very red hair and I spend a lot of money to keep it that way. I won't be seen in public without earrings and make up. I go to an aerobics step class every morning at 6:00 a.m. because I want to wear a size 8 until Jesus comes. I am the Emelda Marcos of Minnesota when it comes to shoes. I do not always color within the lines. I have been known to rip the tags that read, "do no remove under penalty of law" right off the furniture. If there is a shortcut to get where I am going, I am likely to take it. I believe most of the time within the parameters of law and morality, that the end justifies the means. If the end does not justify the means, what exactly does it justify? I strive to tell the truth, but if I can tell the truth in the best possible light to save someone from embarrassment, I will. Just because something is true does not mean that it is worth telling. I can usually see both sides of an issue and as a result I am a very good negotiator. In 1994, I was invited to run on the Republican ticket for Lt. Governor of the state of Minnesota. I did not accept the invitation, but I have always thought I might have been very good at politics because I can usually find a compromise position on just about anything in 30 minutes or less. And in fact, it is the one thing about which I was unwilling to compromise that brought me to the crossroads of my life. That being my absolute belief that Jesus Christ is the Son of God, the Savior of the world and the only way to be reconciled to God the Father. He is not "a" god; He is "the" God. He is not the #1 god in a list of gods. He is the only God. No ifs, no ands, no buts.

As Sergeant Friday used to say, "just the facts, ma'am." So here they are. I was 42 years old and had a career that spanned 20 years in television. I had been the president and general manager of two other stations before I moved to Minneapolis. The CBS station that I managed for 5 years in San Antonio, Texas was voted "one of the 25 best managed television stations in the United States" in 1986. Harte-Hanks Communications owned KENS at that time. KENS was #1 in all news time periods, #1 in prime time and #1 in revenue generation among the 4 stations then owned by Harte-Hanks. The profitability of KENS was greater than the other three stations combined.

The second station that I managed was WTLV, an NBC station in Jacksonville, Florida, but when I moved there in late 1986, it was an ABC station and had the distinction of being one of the worst ABC affiliates in the top 100 markets. In 1987, when the station was sold to Gannett, I presided over the network switch. According to Pierre Mapes, who was then the President of NBC Affiliate Relations, it was the most successful network switch in NBC's history. WTLV rose to the number 2 television station in the market by the end of 1988. WTLV was sold to Gannett in 1987. How that happened is worth a word in this story. In 1986, television stations were hot and were selling rapidly at ridiculously high multiples. I learned that Harte-Hanks, who was primarily a newspaper company, needed cash for another venture and was going to sell their two remaining stations to the highest bidder, keeping only the flagship station in San Antonio. The station in Springfield, Missouri had been sold a year earlier. That meant that because I was in Jacksonville, I was "in play." I was not worried about keeping my job after the sale. I was, however, worried about who the new owners might be. Since I was a corporate vice-president with Harte Hanks, a privately held company of about 35 of us, I knew that the company was not interested in "who" bought the station but "how much" someone was willing to pay. I was the only one who cared who bought the station because I expected to hang around, but no one else in the company cared. In fact, I once had a telephone call with Larry Franklin who was the COO of Harte-Hanks about the management merits of one company over another. His reply to me was, "Try to imagine how little I care."

I learned early in life that the most important decision one can make toward insuring future success is to choose the right set of parents. If I was going to have a new parent company, I wanted to influence the decision. All of the companies, more than 20 as I recall, that were interested in buying the Harte-Hanks stations made arrangements for a due diligence visit to the properties through the home office in San Antonio. All of the visits had to be completed by the middle of November, 1987 because Harte-Hanks wanted to announce a deal before Thanksgiving. I was kept informed as to who all of the prospective buyers were. There was no particular rhyme or reason to which companies got the available appointments. The appointments were arranged on the basis of whom called in first. After the available slots for visits were filled, I got a list of the companies who had expressed an interest and were coming in. But the company that I wanted to work for was not on the list. I wanted to work for Gannett. So, I wrote a letter to Cecil Walker, President of Gannett Broadcasting and told him that the stations were for sale and whether they bought those stations or not, I wanted to work for their company. A few days later, Dan Ehrman, controller for Gannett Broadcasting called me and said that they were interested in the stations. He had talked to San Antonio to try to get a due diligence visit, but was unsuccessful because all of the available slots were taken.

I called the home office and reviewed the list of potential buyers who had appointments and were coming to Jacksonville. On the last available day before the Thanksgiving deadline, Cox Broadcasting was scheduled to come in. I called the offices of Cox and cancelled their appointment. I then called the Harte-Hanks offices and told them that I had cancelled the appointment with Cox and that Gannett was coming instead. Harte-Hanks called and verified that Gannet really was interested and confirmed the visit. Gannett came in and made the winning bid for the two stations. Some have asked why I helped Gannett. I was a corporate vice president and stood to make the same amount per share as any of the other shareholders, who would simply count their money and move on. The staff I had nurtured for two years and I were the only ones who would be subject to the new owners. Was it a bold move for me to initiate the contact with Gannett? Yes, it was. But understand that while taking pre-emptive action without ten layers of ecclesiastical permission in Christian circles may seem unusual and even unsettling to some, there is a different paradigm in private enterprise. Those who are willing to take initiative are highly valued and highly compensated when their initiatives are successful. Harte-Hanks was so pleased with the offer that Gannett made, which was significantly higher than anything else they had received, that Larry Franklin offered me a $100,000 bonus to sign an agreement that I would not leave the company until it had been brought to closing.

Gannett not only asked me to remain in my position as President and General Manager of WTLV, but Cecil Walker confided in me that they had actually paid more for the station than they had intended because of the strength they saw in my management team. When Cecil said that to me, all of my sensors started flashing "larger market." I knew that it would only be a matter of time until I was transferred to one of Gannett's larger and more important television markets. I could hardly wait.

Gannett transferred me to KARE in Minneapolis in May 1989, two years after the acquisition of WTLV. This is important to this story because you should know that I had been well tested by Gannett as to whether or not I fit into their culture and plans before they risked transferring me to a much larger market. In the two and one half years that I was at KARE, I did a pretty good job if ratings and revenue are the indicators of a good job. In the business of television, they are the only indicators. During my watch, KARE improved its ratings to number one in news and its profitability to the second highest in the group of 10 stations owned at that time.

It is important to say that there are many factors that go into making a television station successful including timing and what the world calls luck. Larry Franklin, the Chief Operating Office of Harte-Hanks in 1986, once told me that if given a choice between being smart and being lucky; choose lucky every time. In some ways, he was right. A lot of the success of the stations I had managed was a result of perfect timing on someone's part. Timing is not everything, of course. In addition to timing, there is a lot of hard work involved. As such, there were many people who participated in the growth of these stations. I was not a one-woman show. The best decisions I ever made were to hire people who were smarter than I was and then to take the credit for what they did.

This story would not be a story if I had not had a high profile in the media. Therefore, I have to explain why my profile was high, although my credentials sound more impressive than they actually were. I was one of only 4 women General Managers of television stations in the country at that time and the only one in Gannett. I was listed in "Who's Who of American Women" and was elected as one of the "Outstanding Young Women of America." I was the winner of the YWCA Tribute to Women in International Business award in 1985. I was on the board of directors for the National Association of Television Programming Executives and had been a past president of a chapter of American Women in Radio and Television. I was a frequent conference speaker at industry events. I was a competent and seasoned television executive. My annual income exceeded $250,000. The fact that I was also a deeply committed believer in Jesus Christ may have seemed curious to some considering my position in the media, but to me, I was certain that this was the reason that everything I touched seemed to prosper. It is hard to imagine how things could have been any better or my future more promising than it seemed in 1991.

Then in August of 1991, I surprised almost everyone I knew by resigning my position at KARE-TV and walking away from the job that I had worked my whole life to get. I did it because I refused to obey a corporate order that directed me to stop teaching a Bible study at my church and to refrain from speaking in any public forum about my personal faith. I did not make this decision because I had a mid-life crisis. I did not do this because I was a zealot. I did not do this because I wanted to become an EEOC test case. I did not want to become famous. I was not a religious nut.

This is a book about what happened to me and why I made a decision that some thought was courageous and others thought was foolish. Although my life turned upside down as a result of the story I will tell in this book, the events themselves, the ins and outs of who-said-what at the time is not important. What matters is what has happened in the 10 years since I found myself at the crossroads of my life and career. If I could tell this story without ever talking about the specific part that Gannett Broadcasting played in it, I would. Yes, Gannett was insensitive and callous to the deeply held religious beliefs of an employee. But why would they have been otherwise? Paul understood the facts of life when he wrote *1 Cor 2:14 The man without the Spirit does not accept the things that come from the Spirit of God, for they are foolishness to him, and he cannot understand them, because they are spiritually discerned.*

Although I knew stories of Christians who had encountered problems in reconciling their faith to the demands of the marketplace, it simply never crossed my mind that I might one day be one of the stories. Surely, the challenges that followers of Jesus Christ often encounter in the secular marketplace are as old as the book of Acts. Not only are they not new, they themselves are practically cliché. Everyone knows stories of Christian persecution, and how we will all get our reward in the sweet by and by if we persevere. But not nearly enough has been written about the triumph that happens when God gets involved in the here and now. The things that I learned at the crossroads of my life about the nature and faithfulness of God are worth writing down for someone else. It may be helpful to someone who is not as far down this path of life as I am to read that God is completely trustworthy. That God is completely good is not disputed. That in Him there is no darkness at all is not disputed. But, that He orders the footsteps of the righteous and can be trusted? Many would like to believe that, but few actually do.

Many times we Christians are fond of saying that we want "more of God" without having the slightest idea what we are actually asking for. We want more of God in addition to what we already have. Certainly not "instead" of what we already have. If you want to "go with God" that means that you will have to leave the place where you are now. You cannot follow God and stay where you are comfortable at the same time. But be warned. God is a wild ride. When He invites you to follow Him, think it over. Jesus never tried to fool anybody about what is involved in following Him. If He calls you and you go, it is going to cost you something that you think is important. But in return, He is going to give you something you never dreamed of. Following Jesus is not for the faint of heart or for those who demand predictability and certainty. It demands total trust in Him in whom you have believed but have not seen. You will not be able to see where you are going or how this can possibly ever work out. He knows the beginning from the end, but He will only show you one step at a time. If you choose to go with God, buckle your seat belt, take a Dramamine and hang on.

I confess that this story will not help everyone. It is not for the many in the church today who are content to secure their ticket to eternal life while offending absolutely no one with the demands of following Jesus. It is not for those who are content to be "somewhat Christian." This is a story for eagles, warlords, and kings. It is for those who want to change the world. It is for those whom God is calling to an adventure of supernatural proportions. These are the men and women who are right now making difficult faith decisions in a worldly culture that has no interest in and no understanding of those who are guided by a belief in something beyond themselves. This story is for the person who hasn't yet figured out that the *career* decision he supposes himself or herself to be making, is in fact, a *faith* decision. Both kinds of decisions have consequences. But, a faith decision has eternal consequences.

In some ways I am reluctant to finally memorialize this story in a book. Perhaps you wonder why I feel that way. My story has been written about in *Today's Christian Woman, Charisma*, and *Christianity Today*. Chuck Colson told my story on *"Breakpoint."* Channel 38 in Chicago devoted an entire afternoon time slot to the story. It is even part of a book by Miriam Neff, Shattering Our Assumptions and in God is My CEO by Larry Jillian. My story was also told in detail in the trade press in *Broadcasting and Cable* and *Electronic Media.* The *Star Tribune* in Minneapolis and the *Pioneer Press* in St. Paul, as well as most of the weekly papers, reported the story extensively. I have been the cover girl for *Minneapolis/St. Paul*

*Magazine* in the multi-page story of my life, in which they first referred to me as "The Most Powerful Woman in Town." I have been on the front page of *City Business* under a headline of "The Resurrection of Linda Rios Brook."

My story has not been a secret. So why have I chosen now to tell it myself in a book and at the same time say that I am reluctant to do so? It is because I am truly embarrassed as to how some people tend to react when others have told my story. I tend to be credited with much more courage than I actually have. People who hear my story congratulate me on being willing to pay a high price for my faith. They reflect on the suffering and the loss and they hope desperately that it never happens to them. They insist that I am a heroine of the faith. They are wrong. I have not always known that they are wrong, but I know it now. In fact, for a while, I might have believed my own press about my courage and my suffering for my faith. But over these ten years something else has happened in my life. I have met people who *really have* suffered for their faith. I have met people of remarkable courage and a willingness to sacrifice everything they had and everything they were for the cause of Christ. My story was news because it involved a high profile person in the media. Yes, it was tough. Yes, it was unfair. Yes, I suffered. It was the hardest and worst time of my life. But was it on par with people who lay down their lives for their faith? Not even close.

There is another reason that I want to tell this story. It is to address a question that inevitably arises from people who know the participants in the story. It is a question to which I do not have a fully satisfactory answer, although I shall try to give the best one I have. Since my very public confrontation with Gannett over my personal faith, other people in the organization have been more or less "outed" because they also suffered from being followers of Jesus. Lee Webb, who was an anchor at the Gannett television station in Jacksonville, Florida was ultimately fired for having given a personal testimony of faith at a noon service club meeting in which he shared how his faith impacted his job. Today, Lee is an anchor for the news operation of the 700 Club. However, except for that incident, I am unaware if anyone else has ever been penalized or threatened with penalty for their public activities where the issue of faith has arisen.

For example, in the Twin Cities, it is commonly known that Diana Pierce, also a news anchor who worked at KARE –11 when I was there, is also a "known" Christian and frequently sings songs of faith at public gatherings. I am asked why the company took such a rigid position with me and yet have seemed to ignore Diana's public concerts where she speaks of her faith in word and music. I suspect that there are two reasons. One reason is natural and reasonable. The other reason is spiritual and is probably behind the one that appears natural.

Let me explain them in that order. I was successful with Gannett until 1991 because I was the best kind of employee: an obedient company soldier. I was low maintenance. I was completely loyal to the company and completely predictable. The company issued an order and I carried it out. Regardless of my personal feelings about the order, I obeyed. Every company has politics. I never questioned the politics of any company decision. I fired people who should not have been fired but who had become inconvenient. I hired people who should not have been hired if competency had been the criteria. There was no reason for anyone to suspect that there was anything the company would order me to do which I would refuse to obey. That is how one gets ahead in a large corporation. Obedience and complete loyalty are much more valued than entrepreneurial spirit, no matter how enterprising that spirit might be.

In fact, perhaps this would be a good place to suggest that entrepreneurial sorts might want to get over the idea that large corporations are always looking for people who think for themselves and are willing to challenge the company's position and political line. No, they are not. Private, entrepreneurial business is looking for those kinds of people. Dot Coms are looking for those kinds of people. Large, traditional corporations generally are not. They are looking for people who walk the walk and talk the talk and never step out of line. I'm not suggesting that this is either good or bad. It is just the way that it is.

John Curley, CEO of Gannett, gave the company order that changed my life to me personally. In simple one-syllable words, he told me to stop discussing my personal faith in any public setting and to stop teaching the Bible class at my church. Cecil Walker who was the President of Broadcasting, Madelyn Jennings from Human Resources and Ron Townsend, President of Television were all present in the room. I am quite convinced that there was never a question in the mind of anyone there that I would do more than simply obey. I was the kind of employee who was known so well by the most senior of company officers, that they believed it was safe to speak to me in direct and candid language without concern for political correctness. And they were right. For example, Madelyn asked me to explain to them what my religious beliefs were. That is an illegal request. Nonetheless, I told her about my faith in Jesus Christ. She then said to me "Linda, you are one of the highest paid women in Gannett and yet here you are sounding like a loony." If it were not so that they felt they knew me and therefore had no need of couching their words, that conversation would have been handled in an entirely different manner. A Fortune 500 company has enough sophistication and experience to know that one does not dare use inflammatory language to discipline a "problem" employee. Every person informed on issues of affirmative action and the EEOC recognized that the order delivered to me smacked of discrimination on the basis of religion. Not to mention sex and age.

One does not rise to senior management of a media conglomerate by making those kinds of blunders. I believe that John Curley said to me what he said, because it never crossed his mind that I would do anything other than salute and obey. Cecil would have told him that. That was my history. I obeyed. If anyone at Gannett had really believed that things would progress in the unfortunate way that they did, the course would have been altered significantly from the beginning to insulate all participants from a discrimination suit.

Some have speculated that perhaps the company really thought I was not doing a good job in Minneapolis and wanted a reason to get rid of me and used my Christian profile as a reason. That simply is not true. There is no evidence of any sort to support such a supposition. But even if that were the case that isn't how it's done for a high profile person. The person is given a warning that is placed into his or her personnel file. Six months later the person is quietly dismissed on some other defensible and arbitrary basis, such as failure to meet budget or not gaining enough in the ratings. It's done quietly. Sometimes the employee is retained as a "consultant" for a predetermined period of time. The company does not issue illegal and controversial orders with "lawsuit" written all over them. It doesn't happen.

Why did it get so out of hand? Here is my theory. I have worked my entire life for very powerful and brilliant people. All of who have been men. My experience has convinced me that there is often an Achilles heel with powerful men. They cannot back up. Once a muscle has been flexed and a declaration of power has been made in front of witnesses, some men will risk a bullet before they will back down. John Curley had given me a direct order. There were witnesses. Those who insist on believing that I acted with Herculean courage should know that I tried every way I could think of to find a compromise position.

I could not agree to stop speaking about my faith, but I did offer to submit outlines of the classes I taught and the speeches I made. I felt that once they knew how innocuous my teachings were, that they would realize that this did not merit the kind of attention it was getting. All of the Christian meetings to which I was invited were on weekends, well away from company time. I offered to discuss these engagements where I was invited before I accepted them. But men like John Curley do not compromise when they have issued an order. There were witnesses, after all. In the end, no compromise was acceptable and after days of deliberation, I responded that I could not obey the order.

This is one of the differences that I believe exists between men and women in positions of power. I have often privately believed that if a woman had been the CEO of Gannett, that this tempest in a teapot would have been diffused early on. Women in power whom I have known are generally not governed by the same machismo as men. When red flags begin to wave, women are far more interested in a satisfactory outcome than in who wins a wrestling match of egos.

As I said, I believe the more important reason that things progressed as they did is a spiritual matter. Does that imply that I believe that John Curley or others at Gannett were biased against Christians? No, I don't really think so. It is certainly possible, but I do not think that was the case. I believe that the attention that had come to me as a result of my willingness to talk publicly about my faith was simply an annoyance to the company. It wasn't uniform behavior. Not only was I already different from the other television general managers because I was a woman, but a "religious" woman. That caused people to be curious about me. The company treated this annoying behavior the way they would treat someone who drank too much or used politically incorrect language. They ordered the behavior to stop. I am quite certain that no one at that time had any idea what such an order to be silent about one's faith meant to a Christian.

Gannett almost certainly thought the matter was an issue of obedience to company policy. I was the only one who knew that it was a spiritual matter of extraordinary proportions for me. I have observed that many, if not all, supernatural events are in fact carried out through the appearance of natural phenomena. For example, if you ask a Christian if God judged the sin of the world when He caused it to rain for 40 days and 40 nights, saving only Noah and his family, the Christian would answer "yes." Suppose it were possible for us to ask an independent observer of the flood, one who had no predisposition to believe in supernatural events, whether or not the rain meant that God had judged the sin of the world. That person would likely answer, "No, the weather turned bad." One does not comprehend the spiritual cause of what appears to be a natural occurrence unless he has spiritual eyes to see it.

Therefore, I sincerely believe that the real reason things happened as they did in my life is a spiritual matter. This was the sacrifice God required of me if I wanted to go with Him on a wild ride. I do not know why He hasn't required the same from other people. It is like the story of Peter in the last chapter of John.

*John 21:15 When they had finished eating, Jesus said to Simon Peter, "Simon son of John, do you truly love me more than these?" "Yes, Lord," he said, "you know that I love you." Jesus said, "Feed my lambs."*
*John 21:16 Again Jesus said, "Simon son of John, do you truly love me?" He answered, "Yes, Lord, you know that I love you." Jesus said, "Take care of my sheep."*
*John 21:17 The third time he said to him, "Simon son of John, do you love me?" Peter was hurt because Jesus asked him the third time, "Do you*

*love me?" He said, "Lord, you know all things; you know that I love you." Jesus said, "Feed my sheep.*

It helps to understand the significance of what is going on here if we remember that Peter was the one who had bragged about how he would never deny Jesus. Even if all others forsook Him, Peter would not. Of course, we know that Peter denied Jesus 3 times before the night had ended. Now, in this post resurrection episode, Jesus asks Peter 3 times whether or not Peter now truly loves Him. Peter says that he does and He is redeemed. Which I think would be a perfectly good place to end the story. Instead, Jesus goes on to tell Peter what it would cost to follow Him and to feed the lambs as Jesus had commanded.

*John 21:18 I tell you the truth, when you were younger you dressed yourself and went where you wanted; but when you are old you will stretch out your hands, and someone else will dress you and lead you where you do not want to go.*
*John 21:19 Jesus said this to indicate the kind of death by which Peter would glorify God. Then he said to him, "Follow me!"*

Up until 1991, I was probably more like Peter than I had ever imagined. I was quite bold in telling people how much I loved Jesus and how I would follow no matter what. But that bold profession of faith had never really been tested. August of 1991 made me realize that there is a cost associated with following Jesus. I do not know if there is a cost in *believing* in Jesus. I rather doubt it. But there is a cost in *following* Jesus. Why? A person who believes, but does not follow, is of precious little interest to the devil. Satan, I believe, really does not get bummed out over the salvation of an individual soul. He simply doesn't care that much about individuals. Because we know that Jesus cares about us as individuals, we flatter ourselves into thinking that when we are saved we are some great loss to the kingdom of Hell.

I don't think that Satan wastes his energy on believers who are just believers. Many believers that I have known live lives that would be of very little interest to the forces of evil. On the other hand, I think Satan becomes furious when a *believer* becomes a *follower*. When a believer becomes a follower of Jesus, then he becomes a *carrier* of the faith. His faith now becomes contagious. Satan will react to that. Carriers must be stopped. I rather believe that the names of *"believers"* in Jesus are quite unknown in Hell. But the *"followers"* of Jesus? Their names are on the "most wanted" posters in Hell.

Peter was told in advance what the cost of his "followship" would be. So was I. I was not fired. The company did not "do" something to me. Cecil Walker said to me "You can go a long way in the company, but you must choose. You can do either one. But, you cannot be a Bible teacher on Sundays and an executive for Gannett at the same time."

Peter, having learned what lay ahead of him, turned around and saw John standing by. *John 21:20 Peter turned and saw that the disciple whom Jesus loved was following them. (This was the one who had leaned back against Jesus at the supper and had said, "Lord, who is going to betray you?") John 21:21 When Peter saw him, he asked, "Lord, what about him?"*

*John 21:22 Jesus answered, "If I want him to remain alive until I return, what is that to you? You must follow me."*

We are all like Peter in this way. If we are going to have to suffer, we want to know who else will have to suffer as much. It is cliché to say that misery loves company, but it is also true. I do not know why others have not been required to pay the same kind of price I paid for my public confession of faith in Jesus. I have wondered to the Lord, but I haven't had the nerve to ask Him. Perhaps it is because I know what His answer would be. "What is that to you? You must follow me."

If it were possible to do, I would tell this story without talking about Gannett at all. Because contrary to popular opinion, I really do not hold any ill feelings about the company. I am a natural born capitalist and I respect the right of every private business to make whatever rules it believes to be important to its success. Gannett acted on the basis of what that company believed to be right. I did the same thing. As Cecil Walker was fond of saying, "reasonable people disagree." That is why I did not sue anybody, although the Rutherford Institute contacted me to say that they would be interested in representing me if I chose to do so. And in fact, less than a year after my departure from the company I testified in court on Gannett's behalf in an age discrimination suit brought against them by another employee.

Contrary to what many people think, my story is not about freedom of speech or freedom of religion or discrimination of any caliber. It isn't even about how unfair life is. My story is about choice. It is not about what someone *did to me*. It's about what *I did* at the crossroads of my life. And why I did it. Perhaps "why" is a good place to start.

# Chapter 2

## Wake Me When It's Over

Our family had a dog-named Kahlua. He was the dumbest animal who ever lived. Kahlua woke up in a wonderfully new world every day. It was a world void of any unpleasant experiential baggage. By that I mean that, although he was supposed to have above average intelligence according to the doggie charts, Kahlua neither learned any lesson nor retained any memory from one day to the next. Kahlua's life was like a rented movie that gets caught in the rewind/play cycle of the VCR. It plays out a scene, rewinds and replays the same scene over and over. The main character remains surprised and amazed at what is happening to him, no matter that it has happened 500 times before. Kahlua was a dog caught in the rewind cycle of life. He was always in trouble always for the same behavior. Always punished. And always surprised that anyone was mad at him. The ritual went like this: one of the family members would open the garage door before the kitchen door had closed completely and Kahlua would bolt like a small white tornado. The guilty door opener would then chase him down the street, put a leash on him and scold him all the way back to the house.

Although he was a small dog, a Llaso/Poo, he was not a Romans 12:3 kind of critter in that he thought more highly of himself than he thought. All of the neighbors who also had dogs, had installed invisible fencing to keep their bull dogs, German Shepherds, Rottweilers, etc in their respective yards. Our neighbors obviously had real dogs; real big dogs. We had the village idiot of dogdom.

When little Kahlua escaped, he would run from first one house then to another, going up to the edge of the yard and barking loudly at the dog that lived there. The dog at that house would then charge Kahlua, only to be stopped short at the invisible, electronic fence. Kahlua, of course, thought the animal had drawn back in fear of Llaso/Poo machismo. This in turn caused the agitated animal to run back and forth barking relentlessly at Kahlua, who stood just outside of the fence, satisfied that somehow his prowess had kept the other animal at bay. By the time we could actually catch up with Kahlua, he would have successfully set off a symphony of barking dogs covering two square blocks of suburbia. This was very annoying to the other dog owners. Ultimately, our dog was solely responsible for an ordinance against dog barking in Plymouth, Minnesota. Unfortunately, that wasn't the end of Kahlua's excellent adventure. He would then dash to the playground and proceed to terrorize short children by chewing on their socks while they were wearing them. This in turn tended to traumatize the young inexperienced mothers, who did not appreciate the humor and who tended to get really loud and unpleasant about the whole thing.

Teaching Kahlua not to do this became a high priority for the family. After dragging the dog home, the catcher -of -the -day would spank the dog, show him the door and do exactly what the how-to-train-your-pet-at-home book said we should do. The next day, someone would open the garage door before the kitchen door closed and Kahlua would bolt and the entire episode repeated again. Experience was completely wasted on that dog.

In theory, people are smarter than dogs. We are expected to learn today's lessons to avoid redundant living tomorrow. If Life were fair, eventually we should be able to predict cause and effect. If it doesn't come automatically with age, then surely it should come with experience. Eventually, we should learn to see Life coming. Before Life surprises us with a body slam, there ought to be rules of engagement. People who do not make trouble, look for trouble, or cause trouble, ought to be safe from trouble. That should be one of the rules. The next rule should be that Life itself should obey the rules. But Life does not.

Life simply happens. Unlike tornadoes that sometimes happen in empty fields leaving no casualties, when Life happens, it always happens *to* someone. Life happens without regard for one's carefully thought out career plans. Life happens without regard to current obligations. Life happens while we are getting ready and always before we *are* ready. Life happens to the just and the unjust.

Here's one way to tell when Life is happening to you. You find yourself saying things like, " just wait till things get back to normal." It is because you haven't figured out yet that there is now a new definition of normal. Things aren't going to be "normal" the way they were again. When Life happens, it brings choices. Choice, by the way, is highly over-rated. Think about it. Choices are not benign opportunities about which we can take action or not take action. Choices demand action. If we do not choose, we still choose. Choice demands that we must choose between two things. We can have one or the other; but we cannot have them both. We can have *either,* but we cannot choose *neither.* When Life happens, it is rarely a choice between something good and something bad. That isn't the way it is at all.

Bozo the clown can choose between something good and something bad. When Life happens, the choice is almost always between something bad and something worse.

That difference, between something bad and something worse, is not so easily discerned. And when Life happens, the faster the choices come at us. We do not have enough time to weigh the options. We do not have enough time to consider all of the consequences. We do not have time to seek alternatives to those choices that have come to us unannounced and now demand to be made. The faster they come, the greater the stakes represented by those choices. As the stakes get higher, with it comes the fear of making the wrong choice.

I know something about that kind of fear. It is fear way beyond the casual anxiety that is epidemic in America, creating an entire new industry of mood elevating drugs. The kind of fear I'm talking about is not subtle. It flashes in the mind and then burns slowly down the throat until it lies like coals in your gut. Fear of sudden irretrievable loss. Fear of failure. Fear of looking foolish. Fear of making fatal choices. This is the kind of fear that comes upon people whom others often think of as "fear-less."

I've been told that I am one of those people who appear to others to be fearless. My daughter Kirsten once wrote a paper in her English class in which she was required to use one word to describe each or her parents. "Fearless" is the word she used for me. I look in the mirror and I can't see it myself, but others have said to me so many times that I can be intimidating, that I assume there must be something to what they say. My father used to remark, "If 3 people tell you that you look sick, lie

46

down." Although once people get to know me, I think they rather get over the idea that I might be dangerous in some way. Maybe some have thought me intimidating because I have been the "first woman" in so many instances in my small universe. The "first" anything is always unknown and therefore scary to some that get very nervous when things begin to change. Maybe some considered my apparent success in television to be intimidating. I personally think it has to do with my red hair and Roman nose. In Minnesota, I've been told that red hair is a psychological trigger that causes Norwegians and Swedes to think they have encountered a Viking. As for the nose, just look at how the truly fierce are always portrayed in the movies. They always have prominent noses. Those of us with Romanesque facial appendages could probably qualify as a special interest group. If we could prove discrimination we could probably get government funding. If I am intimidating, as some have said, in addition to the nose and hair, it might be the hats. The nature of my work has often required me to work with groups consisting of powerful men who get the floor, keep the floor and don't let anyone else get a word in. When I realize that I cannot get their attention to share my point of view, I wear a hat. Works like a charm. Abrupt men are much more civilized when dealing with women who wear hats. Being successful means that you get the opportunity to make more of your own decisions. As you climb the ladder of success, there are fewer people above you to make decisions for you. Fewer people to blame when a wrong decision is made. Somewhere near the top rung, you begin to figure out that your destination is not the wide platform of privilege they told you about in business school. It is a trapeze perch from which you are expected to leap. You are on the program to be the next high wire act without a net.

Keeping one's balance on the wire is hard enough but it is not what the crowd paid to see. You must move forward. You must negotiate turns and flips. You must time your moves and choose the correct maneuvers. While dancing on my own high wire, I suddenly contracted the fear that all successful people deny that they have. Fear of waking up one day and finding that I had miscalculated and lost everything I'd worked for because of a wrong choice. Omar Kyam wrote that when Life happens, it's something like this: *"Like one who on a lonely road does walk in fear and dread, and having once turned round walks on and turns no more his head, because he knows a frightful fiend does close behind him tread."* Omar Kyam wasn't the first to discover that life happens. Job said it like this *"That which I greatly feared has come upon me."*

I can remember in Technicolor the day that Life happened to me. I was a reasonably well-balanced conservative woman, who at a pretty good place in her career path, went to bed one night in Plymouth, Minnesota and woke up the next morning in the Twilight Zone. Contrary to what Rod Serling says, there are no signposts up ahead warning you that you are about to enter another dimension. You just step off the wire, and there you are.

******

Whenever a person first realizes that he is dangling on the wire, he begins to review the steps that got him into that predicament. My first questionable choice was in agreeing to move to Minnesota from

Florida in the first place. People always ask me whatever made me think that was a good idea. Let us be clear. It was not my idea. I had been in television for 11 years. I was managing my second television station, WTLV in Jacksonville, Florida. WTLV had been acquired by Gannet Broadcasting and I was excited because I knew that I would have a very promising career with this new company. A friend in the business told me that I was "classic Gannet material" and I believed that I was. And certainly for the first 2 years, it seemed so.

That's how it happened that one day Cecil Walker, President of Gannet Broadcasting, called me and asked me if I was interested in transferring from Jacksonville to a larger market. That's when I knew that it was true. I was classic Gannett and the company had figured it. Obviously I needed a bigger stage. Of course, I was interested. In those days, there was not very much that I would not have done to further my career. Never mind that I had already moved my family from Texas to Florida just two years before. Never mind that my husband, Larry, had given up his job for mine, not once but twice, and now I am going to ask him to do it a 3$^{rd}$ time. Never mind that my children might have difficulty with such a drastic adjustment so close to a prior drastic adjustment. None of that mattered, you see. What mattered was my career. Everyone else would have to adjust.

A reasonable person might wonder just how well my family actually adjusted to my hopping across the country to further my career. When my daughter Kirsten was about 12 years old, I asked her if she thought the neighbors were a little odd. She looked at me in true bewilderment and said, "Mom, we are the oddest people I know." I suppose that at that time in social history, we might have appeared that way. Today it is much more common to see men and families follow the mom's career, but in the 80's, it was still rare and suspicious. Before Larry and I were married, we went through pre-marital counseling in the Episcopal Church. We had both been married once before and we were very concerned that statistically we could be at risk if it is true that second marriages break up more frequently than first marriages. In our counseling sessions, the priest pointed out that the day would come when we would be forced to choose between Larry's career and mine. He suggested that we plan how to cross that bridge before we ever came to it.

In addition to being handsome, talented and funny, Larry often surprises people with his absolute grasp on reality. We went for coffee to discuss what the Priest had said and this was Larry's evaluation of the facts. He said, "What we represent to the world of broadcasting is a vintage '57 Ford and a brand new, fully loaded Cadillac. There are a few collectors who might see the value in the '57 Ford and feel comfortable driving it. But the ones who want to get somewhere fast with flash are going to want the Cadillac." Before we were married, Larry had already resolved in his mind that my career probably had the most mileage in it and that would be the one we would nurture.

To make such a promise is one thing, but how did he feel about the reality? It probably helps if you understand that Larry is the most unthreatened species I have ever known. He has never been envious of, intimidated by, or particularly impressed with anything that I have been about. He has always supported me and never done anything in any way that might have jeopardized my career. Well, except for that one time on "Entertainment Tonight."

When Harte-Hanks sold WTLV to Gannett, we became subject to a new personnel policy concerning spouse travel. Larry and I were scheduled to go together to the National Association of Television Programming Executives in San Francisco. Harte-Hanks had always been quite generous in allowing spouses to travel with their executives, particularly if the executive was a woman. Gannett did not offer the same benefit. Our plane tickets and hotel costs had already been paid by Harte-Hanks before the closing so Larry and I decided that there was no reason for him to stay home since it would not cost Gannett anything and they had not asked me to comply with their policy. We simply had not discussed it. Larry and I decided that what might be prudent would be to avoid making an issue of his attendance at the conference by my attending the Gannett events alone. I suggested and Larry agreed that he should maintain a low profile at this convention until we could discuss the matter with Gannett at another time. Larry had many friends in the broadcasting industry from his years in the business. Larry is also quite social and loves a good party. So while I went to the Gannett cocktail party at one hotel, Larry went to the "Entertainment Tonight" party at another hotel, where they were doing the show live from the convention.

At the Gannett event, suspended from the ceiling were television monitors, each carrying a different syndicated program that was licensed to the Gannett stations in their individual markets. I was standing between my new boss, Cecil Walker, and Pierre Mapes of NBC, both of whom are quite tall and important looking, discussing my delight in being part of Gannett and my wonderful future. When I looked up and saw that the monitor playing just over the heads of the $2^{nd}$ and $3^{rd}$ most important men in my life was tuned to "Entertainment Tonight," I felt a slight shudder. The kind one gets just before he is struck by lightening. They both glanced at the monitor just in time to see my Larry being interviewed on the program about his thoughts on the convention and how television had changed. Having only met Larry once before, and briefly at that, Cecil had the look of someone who knows they are supposed to know the person in front of them, but can't quite place them. Never fear, Pierre Mapes who knew Larry well came to the rescue. "Well, what do you know, there's ol' Larry. I didn't know he was here." Things are fuzzy in my memory after that.

As for the children, our oldest daughter, Daune, was 25 and moved to Florida with us for a few months. Mandy our middle daughter stayed in Houston with her mom and stepfather. Chris and Kirsten who were 15 and 12 moved with us. The ones who might have been at risk for losing-all-my-known-surroundings trauma would have been Chris and Kirsten. Having taken several readings over the years, I am quite convinced that neither suffered from the moves. Had they been timid children, perhaps it would have been otherwise. But both of them had traveled in and around and among interesting places and people as a result of the kind of work I did. Neither of them ever met a stranger and it never crossed their minds that they would not be immediately embraced and cherished in whatever place they were. I would tell you that this is because I am an excellent mother. The truth is that God is an excellent God and full of grace that he lavished upon my family.

Time passed and Cecil forgot about that "Entertainment Tonight" business and one day announced that he was sending me a list of several markets where Gannet owned television stations that might come available for new management in the near future. When it came, I was to read it over and let him know if there were any markets that were of interest to me. When the letter came, he had listed Washington DC, Atlanta, Denver, and Minneapolis as possibilities. I wrote my response that very day. I wrote, "yes" beside Washington DC. I wrote, "yes" beside Atlanta. I wrote, "yes" beside Denver. And I left the line with Minneapolis blank.

Cecil called me a few days later to say that he had received my response. Did I realize that I had not written anything by the Minneapolis opportunity? (Apparently, he did not know that not everyone working in Florida would necessarily view moving to Minnesota as an opportunity. Some might say it was a sentence.) I said that I did in fact realize that I had failed to note anything beside the Minnesota opportunity, and so he asked me why. I explained to him that I did not think that I would be a very good fit for Minnesota in general. Although I had never been north of the Mason Dixon line, I was certain that I knew enough about Minnesota to have valid concerns that I might have nothing of real value to offer there. So he asked me to explain what those things were.

I thought it was obvious. To start with, I was active in my church in Florida, but I was not a Lutheran. I knew of no successful Minnesotans who were not Lutheran. I'd listened to Garrison Keeler so, of course, I knew all about it. Furthermore, I was a conservative Republican. I had it on good authority that the only thing worse than not being a Lutheran Democrat was being a fundamental Republican. But there was more. I had heard about the phenomena known as "Minnesota nice," a ritual in which two people talk but never actually say anything.

It is a game in a way, but when a person isn't a native, he doesn't always know when the game is being played. Suppose for example that I am from Minnesota and you are not. You state your opinion and then ask me for mine. I smile at you and comment on the weather. You conclude, therefore, that we must be in agreement. You leave the room thinking that because agreement has been reached, that a path of action is imminent. I leave the room knowing that nothing of the kind has occurred and that it will be several days before you figure out that absolutely nothing is going to happen. One of the longest playing comedies in Minnesota is at the Plymouth Playhouse and is based on the niceness phenomena that is part of the mystique of Minnesota. The play is entitled "How to Speak Minnesotan." It plays every night to sold out crowds of Minnesotans who laugh out loud at this part of their culture. Texans brag about being big. Minnesotans brag about being nice.

I tried to remind Cecil that, being from the southwest, I had a natural bent toward candor. Meaning that what had made me successful in my career, the ability to speak unadorned plain language, was not likely to be appreciated as a virtue in Minnesota. In fact, I did not think that

Minnesotans were at all likely to warm up to an uppity red head from the south.

He listened carefully and then said to me, "I hear you completely. But what would you think about going to Minnesota anyway?" I said that I did not think much of it and if it were all the same to him, I'd hold out for Denver. Cecil then told me that he hoped I would reconsider because my new job was going to be in Minnesota. Before I accepted, I wanted a few days to think it over. The truth was, I wanted a few days to see if I could find something better.

******

And I almost did. I learned that another company by the name of Smith Broadcasting, owners of a group of small to mid-size stations, was interviewing for a President/CEO position over 5 of their markets. I sent my resume to them and was contacted by them and invited to come to Boca Raton for an interview. The interview went quite well and I felt sure that they would offer me the position. Although it would still require a move, I knew that my family would be much more receptive to moving 300 miles south and remaining in Florida than they would be to living in an igloo in Minnesota, which I was sure would be the case.

A few days after I had returned from Boca to Jacksonville from my interview, the man with whom I had met, Paul Brissette, called me. He said that they were very excited that I was interested in joining their company. He then said that he realized that he had completely forgotten to mention one detail and that he hoped it wouldn't affect my enthusiasm. Smith Broadcasting would be changing the location of their corporate offices from

Boca Raton to Minneapolis and that would be where I would be located.

I stayed with Gannett. If I was destined to move to Minnesota, despite my best scheming to do otherwise, better to go with the devil I knew than the devil I didn't know. Forty-five days later, my husband, my kids, my cats, and my dog had left the place where we were welcomed, admired and liked, to begin a trek across a desert. Of course, I didn't know it was the desert at that time. I can read a map. To most, Minnesota would not normally be associated with a desert. But that is what it was for me. It would be a time of the most significant spiritual testing I had ever imagined.

People have asked my why I moved if I did not want to do it. The answer is simple. At that time, I was a well-trained, company soldier. A soldier may have an opinion, but a soldier takes orders. But how did I convince Larry and the kids that this was a good idea? As I said earlier, Larry and I had agreed from the beginning that whoever's career was escalating would be the career path we would follow. Larry was truly never threatened that the possibility existed that it might be my career. Having made that decision before we were married, when reality arrived, we were prepared to deal with it.

Larry and I both are also blessed with the gift of rationalization. Once we understand what the situation is and that we cannot change it, it only takes us a couple of hours as a team to convince ourselves and others that what has occurred is exactly what we wanted all along. We were so good at it that Chris and Kirsten were convinced that we were moving to a winter wonderland. We are so good at it, we convinced Cecil Walker that we could hardly wait to go. So good were we that by the time Cecil announced to the television group that I was moving to Minnesota and one of the other managers asked why, he answered, "Larry and Linda have always had a fondness for Minnesota." The fact that neither of us had ever been to Minnesota had become totally irrelevant.

Moreover, as I said, there was very little that I would not do to further my career. At least that is why I thought I had moved. Ten years of perspective has shown me something completely different. When I told my family about the job with Smith Broadcasting, my son Chris, who was 16 at the time, said, "So, Mom, we have a choice between Minneapolis and Minneapolis. Why does God want us in Minneapolis?" (I should have realized that his question was prophetic, but what really important person pays any attention to a 16-year-old?) Chris was right. It was not the job that Gannett had for me in Minnesota that caused me to move. It was the job God had for me in Minnesota that moved me there. Gannett was just the cover story that the Lord used to get me to go.

He does things like that, you know. God will work through our natural desires and proclivities to get us where He wants us to be. It is for his purposes, not ours as we often think. Is God, therefore, a manipulator? Of people, He is not, but of circumstances, yes, I think one could make a case that He is. God has been known to take extraordinary steps to get people where He needs them to be, whether or not they are anxious to go. Look at Jonah.

One fine day, the Lord God spoke to Jonah and said *Jonah 1:2 "Go to the great city of Nineveh*

*and preach against it, because its wickedness has come up before me."*
*Jonah 1:3 But Jonah ran away from the LORD and headed for Tarshish. He went down to Joppa, where he found a ship bound for that port. After paying the fare, he went aboard and sailed for Tarshish to flee from the LORD.*

Why did Jonah flee rather than obey the Lord? Because the worst job in the kingdom is the job of prophet. A prophet's job is to speak the word of the Lord to warn the people that judgment is imminent. If the people repent and the Lord relents, the prophet always looks like a failure. Jonah did not know whether the people in Ninevah would repent or not, but he did know the nature of the Lord. Although, scripture doesn't actually say, my guess is that Jonah had been down this road with the Lord before. So Jonah ran away. Didn't work.

*Jonah 1:4 Then the LORD sent a great wind on the sea, and such a violent storm arose that the ship threatened to break up.*
*Jonah 1:5 All the sailors were afraid and each cried out to his own god. And they threw the cargo into the sea to lighten the ship. But Jonah had gone below deck, where he lay down and fell into a deep sleep.*
*Jonah 1:6 The captain went to him and said, "How can you sleep? Get up and call on your god! Maybe he will take notice of us, and we will not perish."*

The men are suspicious that somehow this might be Jonah's fault since he had already hinted that he was running away from God. Jonah confesses that this is probably happening because

58

the Lord God is really annoyed with him. The men try to row back to shore, but the storm gets worse. Reluctantly, they take Jonah up on his suggestion that they thrown him into the sea and be done with him.

*Jonah 1:15 Then they took Jonah and threw him overboard, and the raging sea grew calm.*
*Jonah 1:16 At this the men greatly feared the LORD, and they offered a sacrifice to the LORD and made vows to him.*
*Jonah 1:17 But the LORD provided a great fish to swallow Jonah, and Jonah was inside the fish three days and three nights.*

There is nothing like a change of location to give one a different perspective on life. *Jonah 2:1 From inside the fish Jonah prayed to the LORD his God.*
Jonah repented and asked the Lord to save him. *Jonah 2:10 And the LORD commanded the fish, and it vomited Jonah onto dry land.*
Jonah went to Ninevah and said what the Lord had told him to say. *Jonah 3:4 On the first day, Jonah started into the city. He proclaimed: "Forty more days and Nineveh will be overturned."*
*Jonah 3:5 The Ninevites believed God. They declared a fast, and all of them, from the greatest to the least, put on sackcloth.*
*Jonah 3:6 When the news reached the king of Nineveh, he rose from his throne, took off his royal robes, covered himself with sackcloth and sat down in the dust.*
*Jonah 3:7 Then he issued a proclamation in Nineveh: "By the decree of the king and his nobles:*

*Do not let any man or beast, herd or flock, taste anything; do not let them eat or drink.*
*Jonah 3:8 But let man and beast be covered with sackcloth. Let everyone call urgently on God. Let them give up their evil ways and their violence.*
*Jonah 3:9 Who knows? God may yet relent and with compassion turn from his fierce anger so that we will not perish."*
*Jonah 3:10 When God saw what they did and how they turned from their evil ways, he had compassion and did not bring upon them the destruction he had threatened.*

And, of course, what Jonah feared would happen, happened. The Lord relented. And Jonah was not even a little bit happy about it. *Jonah 4:1 But Jonah was greatly displeased and became angry.*
*Jonah 4:2 He prayed to the LORD, "O LORD, is this not what I said when I was still at home? That is why I was so quick to flee to Tarshish. I knew that you are a gracious and compassionate God, slow to anger and abounding in love, a God who relents from sending calamity.*

Those who decide to move from believer *in*, to follower *of* Jesus Christ will eventually utter those famous words of the true converts; "I'll go where you want me to go. I'll do what you want me to do." When we do that, we usually don't really mean it and take in for granted that the Lord knows that we aren't serious, just momentarily infatuated with our own spirituality. Oh, of course, we mean it at the time. Like when we say to a casual acquaintance that we pray for him every day. No one believes that we actually do it.

I've become convinced, however, that when we say those words to Jesus, He apparently does think we mean it. He sets the Holy Spirit in motion to begin to manipulate our circumstances to get us to the place God wants us to be for the work He has in mind. The work that we so eagerly volunteered to do when we thought He knew we were just kidding. The Lord moved me to Minnesota by offering that I would be the first woman to take over one of the most powerful jobs in local television in the major markets. Naturally, I couldn't wait to go. But what would I have done if He had said to me, *"Look, Linda, what I really want you to do is go to Minneapolis, become publicly humiliated, leave a position of power and influence and take on a broken down television station that no one who can get a real job would even consider. And if you obey me, I will make you and everyone who goes with you very wealthy to do even greater work in my Kingdom."* I would have chained myself to a tree in the parking lot if necessary in order to remain in Jacksonville, Florida. It's not that I didn't have faith. It's just not what I had planned to do with my life. Of course I meant it when I said to the Lord that I would go where He wanted me to go. Provided of course that He was going somewhere I had planned to go anyway. The truth is that I would probably have said, "That's really good, Lord, a great plan about the kingdom and all that, but I'm not your girl. I can get wealthy and do good here on my own if I stay at it and I know I can serve the kingdom just fine from my office. You'll be pleased."

I realize that all Abraham needed was a word from the Lord, "Go to the place where I will send you," and he packed the camels and went. But not this material girl. I needed a little more incentive than that. So, the Lord gave it to me.

It was two years after I arrived at KARE 11 that the Lord laid all His cards on the table. Yes, I could have that which had brought me to Minnesota. He always gives us a choice and He always honors our choices. I could keep what I had. Stay right where I was, salvation nicely intact. But I believed then and I believe now that my spiritual journey would have stopped right there.

In deliverance ministry, the minister knows that the person who needs to be delivered must desire deliverance in order to be freed. That true desire is not always present. What the person sometimes desires is to be relieved of the pain of the consequences of disobedience. The person may not like who he becomes when the demonic exercises control, but in many cases he does in fact receive perverse pleasure from the sin. Pornography is a good example. No person is proud of the fact that he is a prisoner to a demon of pornography. None-the-less, the pleasure that the consumption of pornographic material affords him will often keep him from seeking deliverance. He has come to depend upon the very thing that holds him captive for his pleasure. Until the person of his own free will orders the demon to go, a deliverance minister cannot cast it out. Deliverance is never a substitute for repentance.

Robert Browning once wrote "O wad some power the giftie gie us to see ourselves as others see us." One of the reasons that I had a deliverance ministry was because I am seldom fooled by appearances. I have a very accurate track record for reading motives in people I barely know. Some say it is spiritual discernment and perhaps it is. Perhaps it is also because some forms of the demonic are so easy to identify. Abuse, addiction, pornography, lust, anger, rejection, fear - these all manifest in clearly discernible ways. But there are other kinds of demons that are much more sophisticated. They may not leave observable marks on the person, and if they do, the marks are often mistaken as badges of accomplishment.

I knew that my decision as to whether or not I would leave Gannett had enormous spiritual consequences for me, but I really did not understand why. I did not have a clue that the work the Lord intended to do in me and through me would require my own willingness to be delivered from demons that I had come to regard as my friends. The demons that influenced me were quite the sophisticated sort. Demons of this type are successful because, they convince us that they are not there. They masquerade as the characteristics found in the truly successful. They are pride, achievement, self-sufficiency, rationalization, individualism, worldly wisdom, and materialism. The Lord Himself purposed to be my deliverer. But before He would cast the demons out, I would have to tell them to go of my own free will. Before I could do that, the Lord would have to teach me to trust Him.

Although no one I knew, Christian or otherwise, would have criticized the decision to simply obey what I was told to do and keep my position at KARE 11, I knew that the Lord was inviting me to leave everything I believed to be important in my life for something that He would not clearly reveal. It was a clear choice and it was all mine. Frankly, being fired would have been much easier. I could have been the victim instead of the fool. There would have been someone to blame for the unfairness of it all. Why should I have to choose between something I had earned and a higher place with the Lord? Why couldn't I have both? Why wasn't there another option? Why was it that my only options were to stay in a place of seeming success and security or, I could take a deep breath and step on the roller coaster with Him into who knows where? I could choose either. But I could not choose both and I could not choose neither. For the first time, I had sympathy for the rich young ruler.

# Chapter 3

## Either, Not Neither

My 15 minutes of fame began, shortly after I had moved to the Twin Cities. I was the President & General Manager of KARE 11. Although there were six other people in the Twin Cities with the same title at the other television stations, as nearly as I could tell, none of them were famous. Everyone knows who the local anchor people are. Everybody knows the weatherman. But nobody knows (or cares) who the general managers are. I've tried to figure out why I became such a lightening rod for the local press. Perhaps it was the fact that I was the only woman in that position. Perhaps it was because I could not seem to get the hang of "Minnesota nice." When I was asked a question, I couldn't avoid giving an answer. Janet Mason, the news director, was forever telling me that when people asked me a question that I told them much more than they wanted to know. Perhaps it was because I just did not take seriously, nor could I imagine that anyone else did, the opinions of gossip columnists and tabloid writers.

In one way, a person has to admire the fact that these newspaper types were so creative in finding something about me worthy of column inches. I am the most average person you will ever meet. Everything about me is average. My height is average. My weight is average. I wear a size "medium" in everything. My shoe size is so average that I can never find shoes at clearance sales because my size sells out first to the rest of the average people. Except for my red hair and Roman nose there is nothing unusual about me unless of course you count that exorcism thing.     My husband Larry and I seldom went out socially.  We were invited to a lot of parties as a result of my position in the media, but we both found media cocktail get togethers boring and rarely attended any.   We were neither politically motivated nor concerned about meeting the right people or being seen in the right places.  I should have simply blended in with community wallpaper.  I was warned that in Minnesota, among certain constituencies, the fact that I was so open about my Christian faith could be a liability.  I admit that I simply did not take the warning seriously.  I considered being a person of faith to be unremarkable in America and who cares anyway?

The first time I saw myself referred to as a "born again Christian" in the local gossip column of the *Star Tribune* was December of 1989.  I did not know that I had been insulted.  I was, however, amazed to read it because in December of 1989, I had barely arrived in town.  I hadn't completely unpacked.  I had not yet found a "home" church.  I had never made a speech anywhere about my faith.  I had never spoken publicly about my faith in any venue.  Well, I did pray over the meal at the station Christmas party, but I was asked to do that by the people in charge of the party.   And I did keep referring to it as a "Christmas" party although Janet had warned me that it was a "holiday" party.  I thought that was just plain silly since the whole place was decorated with Christmas ornaments and if it weren't for Christmas, we would not be having a party.  So when I read in the paper, that I was a "born again" Christian.  I wondered, "How could this person possibly have arrived at that conclusion?  There was not enough evidence to convict me of being a Christian." I passed by the hallway mirror on my way out the door and decided to stop and look to see if I had any markings on my forehead that might have given me away. There were none that I could see. I did not think anything more about it.

I suppose I should have caught a clue that what I thought of as meaningless, really had the makings of a genuine scandal when Janet Mason seemed upset by the newspaper comment. She asked me if I planned to write a rebuttal or a letter to the editor. I thought she was kidding. "Janet, all the writer has accused me of is being a Christian. I don't think I have to apologize for that."

After that blip in the newspaper, it came to pass that many Christian organizations began to call me to invite me to speak at area prayer breakfasts and the like. I also found a small church in Wayzata and began teaching a Bible class for adults on Sunday morning. On rare occasions, I taught counselors at a local crisis clinic how to recognize the symptoms of demonic influence in emotional illness and how to do intervention. I actually stopped doing that soon after that unfortunate episode in Apple Valley. It was becoming clearer and clearer to me that some of the folks who were coming to class to learn how to do deliverance were in need of being delivered themselves. Besides, I assumed that if the public relations people at the station were upset that I had been called "born again" in the newspaper that they would probably pass out if anyone mentioned "demons" in the same paragraph with my name. I was right, of course, eventually that is exactly what happened. And when it did, we practically had to call EMS for the Community Affairs Director.

It was about that time, that a man called me and told me about a group of business people who met together once a week for a prayer meeting at the same church I attended in Wayzata and wanted to know if I would be interested in joining them. I didn't know very many people yet, so said I would, and Larry and I both went.

It was a small evangelical church near Long Lake. A dozen or so people regularly attended the prayer meeting that was held on Wednesday nights. Since so many people at the station had developed coronary stress over the fact that I was now known as "a born again," I hadn't dared tell anyone that the roots of my faith were in the Pentecostal church or that I regularly prayed in tongues. It is not that I was embarrassed by it, but there is just so much that a group of Lutherans can process at one time. Most people thought that my background was in the Episcopal Church, which is partly true. Perhaps I should try to clarify that a bit.

When I was a child, we lived in the Texas oilfield country. My mother and father did not go to church because my father was openly hostile toward organized religion although I have really never known why. My mother was not truly hostile, but she was truly afraid of the church. For reasons that I cannot explain, from the time that I was 7 or 8 years old I wanted to go to church. Finally, when I was 8, a small Baptist church was built across a pasture from where I lived. So I began walking to the church on Sunday mornings. I was able to convince the other kids who lived within a half mile of where I did, to go with me. I also dragged my brother, Tony, along, who was 6. The quality of brother/sister relationships is at their prime when the brother is 6 and the sister is 8. The brother just obeys without any question because the sister is older and knows all kinds of important stuff. It is sort of down hill after that. Actually, getting the others to go was also an easy sell. After the church service, there was always a potluck lunch and all us kids could stay and eat with the church members. There were always 5 or 6 of us little kids and we did this for at least a year. Our Sunday ritual went on until a deacon, or someone like that, finally figured out that we belonged to someone and got a phone number so that he could call our parents. I know that what he intended was for my parents to understand that they were welcome to come to church also. Unfortunately, my father thought we were bothering the nice people and wouldn't let us go anymore.

I still wanted to go to church though, so when I was 11, my grandmother said that she would start taking me to church. That is how I came to be involved in the Assembly of God church. I loved that church and by the time Sunday morning came around, I was ready and anxious to go. Unfortunately, of all the churches that my mother feared, she feared the Pentecostals most of all. Mother told my grandmother that she hoped that if we were going to go to church that it would be one that was civilized. My grandmother told her, "Well, Jerry, we go right past a Baptist church not too far from the shopping center." That satisfied my mother who never really cared about details anyway. And it was the truth. We went right past the Baptist church on our way to the Assembly of God church.

Most of my teenage years, I spent trying to get my mother to make peace with herself and with God and to go to church. My mother and father divorced when I was 12 and I lived with my mother. I never tried very hard to get my father to go to church because he was simply too firm in his opinions and our times together were too limited. But my mother was different. She had a spiritual side to her; it was just hard to find. Finally, Mother's life had come unraveled so many times that when I was 20, she agreed to try the church, since nothing else in her life had helped her with her addictions and self-destructive tendencies. But she did not want to go to any church that was going to make her feel guilty about how rotten her life had become. I listed a few denominational options and she said "no" to all of them.

Finally, I said, "OK, Mother, where will you go to church? She replied, "I'll go to the Catholic Church." I think it is worth saying that as far as I know there had never been a Catholic in our family and that my mother did not have the foggiest idea what the Catholic Church was about. I asked her if she was concerned about the infallibility issue with the Pope. She thought all denominations had some kind of Pope and that they all thought they were infallible so what was the big deal? I think she really picked the Catholic Church because she liked the idea of those little candles. So that is how I became a Catholic. If my mother was finally OK to go to church and it was Catholic, I was OK with the Catholic Church. I liked all the pageantry and I liked the little candles, too. I have also heard some very powerful sermons in the Catholic Church. But I had a nagging concern that I decided I had to share with my mother before we were actually baptized and received as Catholics. What I shared with my mother that day had much less to do with the liturgy of the Catholic Church than it did with my own limited spiritual history and understanding of how things got done where God was involved. It, therefore, should not be viewed as critical of the church's culture. Mother and I went out for coffee and I made her promise me that if I was ever in an accident or really sick, so that I was unable to communicate, that she would not call a priest. Instead I gave her a paper with the names of several Pentecostal pastors on it. When my mother asked me why, I said, "Because by the time a priest can look up the right prayer in his book, I could be dead. I want you to get in touch with someone who can get God on the phone right away." As I said, I did not intend to be critical. But my limited exposure to Catholic priests at that time had never included spontaneous prayer.

I spent the decade of my 20's in the Catholic Church, but when Larry and I decided to get married, I became an Episcopalian because he was one. Further, we had both been married before which was a problem for the Catholic Church. After going through a time of pre-marriage counseling in the Episcopal Church, we were married at Christ Episcopal in San Antonio, Texas and became founding members of the Episcopal Church of the Holy Spirit in the same city. I spent the decade of my 30's in the Episcopal Church. I was an Episcopalian when we moved to Minnesota.

But I never really got over being Pentecostal. And in my years as a Pentecostal, I had been to a lot of prayer meetings. I was very accustomed to seeing people saved, healed and delivered on a regular basis. In a Holy Ghost prayer meeting, we didn't think anything had happened until someone was slain in the Spirit or received "a word." That is why I speak as a person of some knowledge in the matter when I say that the prayer meetings going on at that little church in Wayzata were not a great threat to the spirit world. And they certainly could never have made anyone even a little nervous that the Holy Spirit might show up and do something.

But that was fine with me because I had become convinced that I should just keep my spiritual head down and avoid anything rash. There was this one particular fellow named Randall who also attended the Wednesday night prayer meetings. Randall had the responsibility for a local computer software company. Right away Randall seemed to identify with the particular stresses of my life. The way this prayer meeting worked was that we would each talk about our week and then we would take turns praying for one another. That's how it happened that on this particular night in early 1991, Randall decided to pray for me. I remember it like it was yesterday. How he folded his hands and bowed his head and began to speak in that "church" voice people use when they pray out loud and are afraid they'll make a mistake and then God will smite them. He said "Our heavenly and gracious father, we thank thee for thy bountiful blessings on our sister, Linda." And then he stopped talking. Dead silence. No "amen," no nothing. It gets to be a long time.

It got to be so long, and from all of the fidgeting in seats, it became clear to me that nobody else seemed to know whether to say anything or not. I sat there in perfect compliance with bowed head and closed eyes waiting for somebody else to do something. Finally, it was so quiet; I thought that maybe everyone had left so I opened one eye to check it out.

What to my wondering eyes did appear but Randall, who is now standing up and staring at something on the ceiling. I open the other eye to try to see what he was looking at. I didn't see a thing worthy such intense concentration. Then with no warning whatsoever, Randall came over to me and put his hand on my shoulder. That alone should have been an indication that Randall was about to have a "spell," as my grandmother would say of people who, without warning, slipped off into another dimension. Let it be known that a Christian man in Minnesota does not lay hands upon a woman in a prayer group unless she is a blood relative, or has died and he is helping to carry her out.

I was still amazed at the hand on my shoulder when Randall suddenly began to speak again, but in a very different way. His voice had changed. He spoke the way normal people speak when they are addressing someone whom they know really well. With his hand still on my shoulder, Randall cried out to the ceiling, "Father God." I knew right then there was going to be trouble. "What I really want to ask you to do is to release Linda from the bondage that she is in with her career so that she can be free to do what you really brought her to Minnesota to do. Amen."

I just about passed out from shock. Not only was I certain that my grandmother would have been right that this man had temporarily checked out of reality, but I was very annoyed. And for some strange reason, I was very nervous about what he had said. Where did this man get the idea that he could pray over me for something that was so opposite of what I wanted? I wanted to rebuke him. *"Who asked you to pray anything like that,*

*Randall?"* Instead, I prayed under my breath "cancel that, Lord, cancel that. I do not agree." I knew my Bible. *Mat 18:19 "Again, I tell you that if two of you on earth agree about anything you ask for, it will be done for you by my Father in heaven. Mat 18:20 For where two or three come together in my name, there am I with them."* If it took two or three in agreement before the Lord would answer requests, I wanted to be sure that Jesus knew that He did not have the votes.

I could not wait to get out of there. For the next few days, I was so upset over Randall's prayer that I found it difficult to concentrate on other matters. Some may wonder why. It was because of what I knew about the power of prayer. It works. Don't misunderstand me. It is not as if any person can pray for something to happen to someone else and then it happens just because the person who prays has somehow invoked the supernatural. God will not be manipulated and Christian prayer is not witchcraft or voodoo. One cannot just stick a pin in a doll and curse the person whom the doll represents with "prayer." But, when a Christian is praying *in* the will of God *for* the will of God in the life of another Christian, it works. And the prayers of a righteous man, particularly, availeth much. Sincere prayer that is in agreement with God's will causes things to happen.

I was disturbed that Randall had not asked me if I wanted that kind of prayer. If he had asked me, I would have said "Let's keep it light, Randall. People are getting nervous as it is. Pray that I will do my job well. Pray that I will be successful. Pray that I keep the Ten Commandments. But don't pray anything that might make me appear weirder than people already think I am. And whatever you do,

74

do not even think about touching my career. God's will is for me to be the first woman to be president of a major television group. Pray for that."

The winter passed in an uneventful way, at least it was uneventful for Minnesota. Twenty below still qualified as an event for me, but I was trying to be nonchalant. Things were actually going pretty well except for that 20 below business and by June, I had almost forgotten about Randall's prayer. Then one day, life happened to me.

I found myself as the cover girl for a tabloid newspaper; a weekly called the *City Pages*, known for its counter cultural view of anything traditional or conservative. You can always tell who the readership of a newspaper or magazine is by the kinds of products or services that are advertised in it. *City Pages* was supported primarily from advertising derived from interesting dating services and entertainment establishments. Not the audience, I would assume, that would care very much about the religious activities of a middle-aged woman. None-the-less, the paper had devoted an entire issue to my Christian activities under a banner headline that read "God and Gannet." The article called into question whether or not a fundamentalist Christian should be trusted to manage a television station with a large news operation if she were willing to speak about her personal faith at prayer breakfasts. Especially a Christian who thought she could cast out demons. Up until that line, it was a pretty dull article. I was only upset that they had called me fundamentalist. I thought they should at least get their terms right. I preferred to be known as "spirit filled."

I was always annoyed when a Christian was made to look foolish by the anti-Christian bias of some of the secular media, especially now that it was me. But I was not worried about any long-term effects because I could not really imagine that anyone would take such contrived tripe seriously. Gannett's headquarters were in Washington. Some have wondered how they became aware of the article. I was the one who sent the article to them. That is what you do when you are a company soldier. You send in the good, the bad, and the ugly if you appear in the press.

What happened next is documented in the first chapter of this book. It was not very long before it became public that Gannett had directed me to stop teaching a Bible study at my church and to refrain from speaking about my faith in any public forum. If the Gulf War had not ended a month earlier, this whole matter would likely have come to nothing. But as it was, the war was over and there simply wasn't much going on in the heartland in August of 1991. I was the best story in town and a media feeding frenzy ensued as people speculated as to what I would do.

The makings of a good soap opera were too good for the local media to pass up: a high profile television executive, a woman at that, in a religious war with a powerful media corporation, whose very existence depended upon the preservation of the 1st amendment. The tabloid press was torn. They did not know whom to attack: the "religious right" or "big corporation."

One morning in the midst of it all, as my whole life appeared to be falling apart and I sat staring at my picture on the front page of yet another journalistic wonder, "The Reader," Randall called me. He said to me "Linda, how are things going." And I said, "Oh, just great Randall, don't let all this blood bother you. How are things with you?" And he said, "Linda, I'm just calling to tell you not to worry. This is all going to work out for you because I am praying for you." And I said, "Randall, would you want to just cut that out?"

Life happened to me and it brought those choices I told you about before. A choice between something bad and something worse. And as a result, I resigned from the job I had worked all my life to get. As in any good soap opera, there is a gauntlet to be thrown down. A final moment, beyond which there is no return. So it was for me. After I had informed Cecil Walker that I would not be able to obey the directive given to me by John Curley, I was allowed one more chance to think it over. I was scheduled to speak at the International Lutheran Conference on the Holy Spirit on the following Wednesday morning. My topic was "Called to Holy Worldliness," how Christianity works in the real world. If I cancelled my participation in that, a cooling off period would follow and then things could be expected to return to normal. Whatever normal was.

I did not make my decision in a vacuum. I consulted with three different flavors of official clergy: an evangelical minister, a charismatic minister, and the senior pastor of one of the most influential Lutheran churches in the Twin Cities, Dr. Morris Vaagenes. While all three agreed that there was more going on here than a secular observer could possibly understand, it was Dr. Vaagenes who helped me see it for what it was. It was also Dr. Vaagenes who had invited me to speak at the Holy Spirit Conference and had graciously offered to withdraw the invitation to give me an easy out. In other words, I could get off the hook without losing face with anybody.

Dr. Vaagenes helped me realize that I was at the crossroads of my life. There were two paths before me. I could choose "either" but I could not choose "neither." What did I really believe? God said, "have no other idols (gods) before me." Was my career in position to become a god to me? I began to think it through. What does a false god look like? What does one do for the false god he serves? What is their relationship like?

Scott Peck once wrote that every sane person worships something. I believe that he is right. There are very few true atheists. It is built into the fiber of our beings to seek to connect our spirits to something higher than ourselves. If we do not worship the true God of the universe, then we will worship something else. Whatever kind of idol it may be, the worshipper believes that the false god he has created is responsible for every good thing in his life. His identity is so interwoven with that god that he cannot imagine going on without it. The worshipper's sense of meaning and purpose are subject to the pleasure of his god. The worshipper thinks about his false god all the time. He worries that his god might be lost to him at some point. He will make every decision around protecting that relationship upon which he has become so dependent. As for the false god, he only requires one thing: the sacrifice of everything the worshipper has.

I was facing a decision involving eternal consequences no matter what I did. I was not choosing to obey or disobey a company order. Oh, that it were only that. I was not pitting my first amendment rights against a corporate mandate. It was far more than that for me.

*Josh 24:15   But if serving the LORD seems undesirable to you, then choose for yourselves this day whom you will serve, whether the gods your forefathers served beyond the River, or the gods' of the Amorites, in whose land you are living. But as for me and my household, we will serve the LORD."*

I was choosing that day which God I would follow and which God I would serve.   The consequences of that decision were eternal.   I know it now and I knew it then.   Nothing less could possibly have led me to take the action I did.   I spoke at the Holy Spirit conference and walked away from every bit of success and security I had ever known.

I don't think it is possible for anyone to really know what my job meant to me without knowing why it meant so much.   While I have written a little about my home life, I haven't come close to describing it as it really was.   When I was 12 years old, I learned the golden rule.   He who has the gold makes the rules.   If you don't have any gold, you live according to somebody else's rules.   My parents were divorced that year and I learned what it meant to lose all the gold.

After the divorce, I lived with my mother and stepfather who had the kind of relationship described in the war rooms of angry nations: mutually assured destruction.   For most of their marriage, the two of them were heavily addicted to alcohol and prescription drugs.   As a result, my stepfather could not keep a job.   We were always poor.   We lived with relatives between the short periods of time when we would have our own place. We never stayed very long because we were evicted several times for failure to make house payments. Our car was repossessed. Both of my parents were arrested more than once for writing bad checks. By the time I was a junior in high school, we lived in a one-bedroom rental house outside of town with no electricity and no water most of the time. By this time, the first of my younger sisters had been born. I was 17.

I did not participate in any activities at school because I did not want anyone to know how my family lived. Our circumstances met the definition of white trash. And it all could have been avoided, if only someone in the family had been willing to work. My parents either could not or would not work and I was too young to get a job. Shortly after turning 17, I moved to Del Rio, Texas to live with my father and brother until I graduated from high school 6 months later and left home. I worked two jobs most of the time, brought my younger sister to live with me and attended school at night. I was determined that I would not repeat my parent's lives. I moved to San Antonio, Texas and got my first job in media, at a radio station, when I was 19. I continued to attend night classes. When I was 21, Neil Armstrong walked on the moon and my mother suffered a complete nervous breakdown. She was hospitalized for a number of months. During that time, my stepfather sobered up and found his first full time job in years. When my mother was released from the hospital, they both moved in with me until they could get on their feet again. We then decided to move to Houston. My stepfather would work, I would go to school at the University of Houston full time, and my mother would take care of both my sisters who were 2 and 3 years old.

In 1971, I left the family in Houston and moved back to San Antonio and got my first job in television at KENS-TV.

There were many others who began in the media when I did who were better educated and more polished than I was. Yet most of them lagged far behind me in promotions and opportunities for advancement. How did I beat the odds of my background (and my gender) to become President and General Manager of the most profitable CBS station in the top 50 markets by the age of 33? I had already figured out that education and talent were not enough to get to the top. If it were enough, there would have been more women at the top. There had to be something else and I thought that I knew what it was. Although as an English major, I had never had any business courses, I did understand something about human behavior. Since humans still ran businesses, I had figured out that what would work for humans, would work for business. And I had learned in life a principle that always seemed to work with humans. The most important problem in the world to a human being is the one he is facing at the moment. If you can solve the problem a person is facing at the moment, big or small – does not matter a bit, you can become a hero with very little effort. I found that it worked very much the same way for business. So, here is how I applied what I thought I knew at KENS-TV and how I moved from being the lowest paid employee in the station to being the President and General Manager in 10 years.

When I returned to San Antonio from Houston, I first tried to get a job in a radio station since that was where my experience was. The first station that I called told me that they did not have any openings, but the man I talked to said that he knew for a fact that the same type of job in television would be coming available at KENS. He knew this because the person who had the job was going to resign the next day. I went down to KENS and applied for a job writing commercials and doing traffic. (When I told my mother that I had a job in traffic, she asked if I got to carry a gun.) Traffic means operations. It is where the commercial and programming log by which a station operates is put together. The sales manager I interviewed with said that KENS had not had any turnover in a while and did not expect any. I asked him if he would keep my phone number just in case something came up. The next day he called me and said, "You'll never believe it, but my best traffic girl just quit." I was properly amazed at the fortuitous timing. After I had been there for 6 months, the manager of the department who had been there for 12 years decided to move to Alaska. I was promoted to the head of the department.

I worked in traffic for 2 years before I was totally burned out on it. The station had a new General Manager named Bill Moll, who would over time become a teacher and mentor to me. But at that time, I was just the traffic girl. There was another position in the station that everyone dreamed about. It was the job of Promotion Director. The promotion department was the toy box of the television station. Promotion Directors got all those neat jobs of arranging network stars' visits, planning parties for advertisers and doing advertising campaigns for the station's newscasts. I wanted a chance at a job like that. But, I was unlikely to get it because I did not have the specific kind of training or experience needed for that position. KENS had experienced a particularly unfortunate run with its Promotion Directors over a decade. There had been 8 people in the job in 10 years. Many of them had simply become overwhelmed with the glamour and lost site of the fact that there was a real job attached. I was in the lobby on my way home one afternoon when the current Promotion Manager called from a conference in New Orleans to tell Bill Moll that she was never coming back. I learned this from Rosie, the operator. I turned around and went to wait outside of Bill's office until he got off the phone with her.

This happened in September, which is the busiest time for the promotion department because of the network new season. As soon as Bill hung up, I walked into his office and asked him if I could do anything for him before I went home. He told me about the loss of yet another Promotion Director. I asked him to let me have the job. He responded, "Linda, you do not know anything about promotion." "That is not quite true," I said. "But more importantly, I do know how this television station works and I know what needs to be done to keep going right now." He agreed to let me do the job until he found the right person for it. Three years later, I was still the Promotion Director.

But by then, I was restless again for a new challenge. I decided that I wanted to produce the news. I asked Bill if I could apply for the opening for a 5 o'clock producer and he said, "No, you are too valuable to the promotion department."
I never disobey. But I did go down to the newsroom and asked the News Director if I could

help out until he hired a new producer. The Assignment Editor was anxious to have a "go-fer" and talked the News Director into letting me help out when I had time. I arranged to have time every afternoon at 3 PM. By the end of a month or so, I was producing the 5 o'clock news by myself and running the promotion department. They had stopped looking for a producer. Although I had by this time been producing the news for over 6 months, I had never actually been given the job. Finally, July 4th came and landed on a Wednesday. July 4th is a holiday for everyone in the television station except for news personnel. Since I was not officially news personnel, I stayed home. At 3:30 the Assignment Editor called me and wanted to know when I was coming in. I told him that I wasn't coming. "That is really not my job. I've just been helping out on my own time." When I arrived at the station the next morning, I was summoned to Bill Moll's office where he and the News Director had been having a chat. I was offered a salary to produce news in addition to my job as Promotion Director.

One year later, I accepted a job as the manager of a local advertising agency. I had not really wanted to leave KENS for a different job. I had planned to grow old and die there as the longest tenured employee at the station. I expected to be buried in the parking lot. But the next level of management for me was beyond my grasp. In those days, women were simply not promoted to the level of Program Manager or Station Manager or beyond. These were decision making positions that determine success or failure and it was territory that was completely male dominated. The Program Manager's job came available at KENS, but Bill would not seriously consider me for it. At the same time, the television station had a very important account in the form of movie theaters. John Santikos owned the largest chain of theaters in the Southwest. He was an important client to the station, but he was also very high maintenance. He owned an advertising agency that handled all of his movie advertising and promotion. But the manager's position in the agency turned over every six months or so because Mr. Santikos was a very volatile, emotional, and brilliant crazy person. Is that an over statement? No, I don't think so. For example, if you were to say the word "cancer" in his presence, he would whip out a can of Lysol and spray you with it.

Bob Polunsky was the Local Sales Manager at the television station and the designated keeper of the Santikos account. When John Santikos had a problem, Bob Polunsky had a problem. If Santikos could not find a manager for his advertising agency, it became Bob Polunsky's problem. That's how it came to be that Bob promised to help find a new manager for the agency. Unfortunately, the reputation of the Santikos agency was widely known and no one with any real credentials would apply for the job. That is why Bob came to me and asked me to apply for the job. I did not want the job. I had a job. Bob was upset because Mr. Santikos had cancelled all of his movie advertising and vowed not to restore it until he had a manager in place to take care of it. KENS had lost a huge amount of billing. Bob assured me that I didn't have to take the job, but if I could interview and appear interested, perhaps that would buy him some time to try to find someone else who would take the job. Bob said he would take me to lunch afterward, so I agreed.

I went to interview with John Santikos at his house. He was at his house because his housekeeper had quit and he had tried to load his dishwasher by himself. He placed a dozen long stemmed wine glasses on the top shelf of the dishwasher and slammed it closed. Of course that action sheared off the stems of the glasses and sent glass flying everywhere. I got there in time to find him hopping around the kitchen holding his bleeding finger and yelling something in Greek. I helped him put a band aid on his finger, cancelled his 911 call and swept up the glass while he took an aspirin and lay down on the sofa. I went in and sat down with him to assure him that he really did not need to go for a tetanus shot and offered to take his temperature and pulse to be on the safe side. Does this sound like a well-balanced person to you?

After an hour of discussing every thing from conspiracy theories to corporate espionage, and never once mentioning anything remotely associated with advertising, Mr. Santikos asked me when I could start work. I said that I could not start because I had a job that I liked very much. He asked me how much I made and then offered to pay me 50% more to come to work for him. I had no intention of doing any such thing, but I was flabbergasted that someone would offer me that much money. When I got back to the station that afternoon and told Bill Moll about it, he looked quite serious and said to me, "Take the job." I was crushed. How could he get along without me? Then Bill said to me, "Linda, you cannot get where you want to go here unless you are willing to go somewhere else first. You grew up here. No one takes you seriously for senior management. Go prove yourself somewhere else." And so I did. I worked for Santikos for one year. It was one of the most fascinating and pleasant experiences I ever had. I learned a great deal about the entertainment business, but more than that, I learned that I was particularly gifted in managing eccentric people. I was very happy with what I was doing and I only left because of the phone call I received one September morning.

One year from the day I left KENS to go to work for John Santikos, Bill Moll called me and offered me the Program Manager's job at KENS. I went on to be Station Manager, the General Manager, then President and General Manager. Not only was I one of the first women to attain such a position, I was also the youngest. I had arrived at respectability, security, money and power. I remembered where I had come from and I was not going back. There was nothing the company I worked for could have asked of me that I would not have done. At least, almost nothing.

When I walked up to the microphone at the Holy Spirit conference, you could have heard the proverbial pin drop. Everyone there had read the papers and knew what I was doing by being there. The tabloid press sat on the right hand side. When I said the words "I am here because I am not ashamed of the gospel of Jesus Christ," the audience rose to its feet, the flashbulbs flashed and the press left. I finished my speech and went home. At the end of the Holy Spirit conference, the radio stations and the press geared up again because they knew that the gauntlet had been thrown down and that Gannett now had the ball. People have asked me what I thought about and what I did that afternoon, knowing that my life in broadcasting was most certainly over.  At least my life as I had come to know it. I went home and gave Kahlua a bath.

# Chapter 4

## What Am I Doing Here?

There is nothing in life that prepares one to be the center attraction in a 3-ring circus. And there is nothing in faith training that prepares us to be humiliated day after day in the media because of our faith. In seminars that I have led on faith building since this whole chapter of my life began, I often ask the participants this question. How many are prepared to die rather than renounce their faith? Nearly every hand in the group goes up. Then I ask another question. How many are prepared to be laughed at by your peers; thought foolish by people whose respect you once had; and humiliated by the media rather than compromise your faith? Not surprisingly, the hands do not go up nearly as quickly. Sometimes, if it is a very honest group, no hands go up at all. Why?

Primarily it is because it is easy to make promises about things that we don't think are ever going to happen. For example, although my son Chris is today a teacher of theology and music in a private school in Texas, after graduating with two degrees, the fact is that when he was a child in school, I never knew until the last day of the last month of the school year whether or not Chris would be promoted to the next grade. Not only did he suffer from petit mal epilepsy as a child, but he simply could not make the connection between schoolwork and anything else in life. By the time he had reached his senior year in high school, he was better, but a long way from scholar status. Larry and I had determined early on that while it was necessary for Chris to go to college, it would not be the best use of our capital to send him to anything except a junior college. Imagine our surprise when Chris announced that he wanted to attend Bethel College, a prestigious private school in Minnesota with a tuition schedule to match. Naturally I was not about to discourage my first born by telling him that there were no circumstances under which I would be willing to waste this much money on private education, having just lived through 12 of the most frustrating and stressful years of my life in trying to bring him to graduation from high school.

Instead, what I did was to ask him how he expected to be accepted at Bethel with his grade point average. He did not know. I told him that I would look into it. I called the registrar at Bethel and proceeded to tell them about Chris and his academic achievement so far. Could he get in? The registrar was kind, but informed me that the only two chances he had were slim and none. I thanked him for telling me what I already knew. When I got home that evening, Larry and I told Chris that if he could get accepted to Bethel, then we would pay for his entire tuition. A week later, he went for an interview with the head of the music department. A few days later, Chris came bounding in the door of my office at KARE 11 to tell me that he had been accepted at Bethel. I rejoiced with him at this confirmation that the age of miracles had not passed and the moment he left the room, I quickly called the registrar. "Remember me? I'm the mother of the slim and none boy who had a better chance of being abducted by aliens than getting into Bethel College." He said, "Well, you know normally that would be the case. But Chris came over and so impressed the head of the department that he exercised his option to over ride the normal admission criteria." Of course we were thrilled. The point is that it had been easy to promise Chris that we would pay for this pricey education when we thought there was no possibility that it would happen. Many times, we make extravagant vows to God about what we will do under certain circumstances, knowing perfectly well that such a thing is never going to happen.

In America, we are pretty confident that no one is actually going to take us up on being willing to die for our faith. It is highly unlikely that anyone is going to shoot at us because we are Christian. But we are equally certain that Christians who become public in any significant way are fair game for people who buy ink by the barrel. Some people probably are prepared to die for their faith. Few, however, are prepared to be laughed at because of their faith. As such, we have helped Satan to learn from his mis-assumptions. He made a bad guess in thinking that persecution would cripple the church. In fact, the church has always thrived under persecution. But what persecution could not do to Christians, the threat of humiliation has done quite well, at least in American Christianity. Consider the caricature of Christians in the Pro-life movement as depicted by many secular news sources. The fear and consequences of being portrayed as a bomb-wielding zealot have paralyzed many us from applying Biblical principles to other issues of common morality in the marketplace of ideas.

Unfortunately, the humiliation that came about as a result of my public spectacle was not limited to me. My husband and my children also suffered especially, my daughter Kirsten, who was

15 at the time. It is hard to be 15 years old under the best of circumstances, much less being the daughter of a quasi-celebrity without having that celebrity status change over night from "media executive" to "religious nut." Fifteen-year-olds deeply desire that their parents remain as anonymous as possible and do nothing to embarrass them. It was hard for her to go to high school every day and face her friends who had heard all about her mother from the shock jocks on the local radio station. She coped in an amazing way for 15. Today, I think she is somewhat proud of what I did. But back then, the truth was that she alternated between being mad at me and being mad at God. So did I.

Contrary to what most people thought would happen in my life after my very public crisis between faith and career, I did not sue anybody; I did not write a book; I did not become famous and I did not receive an immediate call to the ministry. I just went back to work. I would like to tell you that I never had a moment's equivocation about my decision to leave KARE 11 but frankly, that isn't true. I had a lot of fear and to be quite honest, things did not appear to be going all that well for me at first. I was probably a little depressed and wondered whether or not I had really taken a stand for my faith or simply committed professional suicide. Even today, people who still have an interest in this story ask me if I made a mistake in walking away. Would Gannet have really fired me if I had just stayed and held my ground? Probably not. They never said they would fire me. They told me to make the choice. I have been criticized for failing to "take them on." If I had just complied for a few months and kept my head down, wouldn't it all have eventually blown over? Maybe. In fact, probably. Contrary to how it seemed at the time, I really was not the most important issue on the corporate burner. I don't know that I have ever made anyone else understand how very little Gannet had to do with any of this. In spite of what they said, it was not Gannet who was forcing me to choose. It was Jesus.

People who know me and are aware of how much I rely on scripture for guidance, are often surprised that the Bible story that influenced my actions the very most was not one about a hero of the faith. It was a story about a failure. It is the story about an otherwise unremarkable civil servant, which would have slipped under history's radar screen except for one encounter. His name was Pilate and his life changed the day he met Jesus.

I have always been interested in why Pilate crucified Jesus. Being someone who has known a lot of powerful people, I am always curious as to why these kinds of people do the things they do. Their motives are rarely obvious. I had read what the Bible tells us about Pilate and Jesus, but I always suspected that there was more to the story. It did not make sense for Pilate to take the action he took. He should have thrown the Sanhedrin and Jesus out on their collective ear. There was no case. The witnesses against Jesus could not even agree with one another. If Roman rule was known for anything, it was known for its justice system. Roman justice was revered for the fact that it was recognized to be impartial and not influenced by local custom. When the Apostle Paul was given a choice between being brought before a court of his Jewish peers or to be brought before a Roman court, he appealed to Rome. The last thing that Pilate should have gotten involved in was some silly religious local dispute. The fact that Pilate acted in a way that was contrary to his position and training, had always caused me to suppose that there was more going on with Pilate and the Sanhedrin than is commonly known. When I studied the matter in more detail, as Paul Harvey would say, I learned the rest of the story.

We only need turn to history, back to the time of Herod the Great to discover why Pilate rejected every precept of Roman law and ordered the execution of a man whom Pilate knew to be innocent of the charges brought against him. When Herod the Great died, he divided his kingdom between his three sons: Philip, Antipas, and Archaleus. Philip and Antipas ruled well, but Archaleus was a train wreck. His jurisdiction included the volatile area of Palestine. Archaleus governed with such tyranny that the Jewish people themselves turned to Rome to bring order and asked the government to establish a procurator over the area to corral Archaleus. Pilate was appointed to this position in 30 AD.

Pilate did not live in Jerusalem. He lived instead in Cesarea. But he came to Jerusalem often and when he did, he would have his soldiers precede him with standards that bore the likeness of the emperor. Procurators before Pilate had not displayed the standards because it needlessly antagonized the Jews who were offended by anything smacking of emperor worship. Pilate, however, held the Jews in very little regard and thought they were foolish, superstitious people. One day Pilate offended the Jews more than usual. When he left Jerusalem to return to Cesarea, an entire contingent of Jewish men and boys began following behind Pilate's entourage, pleading with Pilate to discard the offensive standards. By the time they reached an amphitheater near Cesarea, Pilate was so outraged that he had all of the Jews gathered into the amphitheater where he threatened to kill them if they did not stop harassing him. The Jews tore their clothes and bared their throats and dared Pilate to follow through with his threat.

Pilate's powers of government were extremely limited. He was not even allowed to raise taxes, much less engage in wholesale slaughter. Pilate was forced to back down from his threat. When word of this reached Tiberius the Emperor, Pilate was severely reprimanded and told to get rid of the standards.

Shortly after that incident, Pilate was at work on one of his civic duties, which was to improve the water supply to the city. He wanted to build a new aqueduct but could not raise taxes and did not have the money to do it. So Pilate raided the temple and took money from a fund called Korban, which he knew that the Jews considered tainted money. It was money the Jews paid in to compensate for sins. It was therefore unusable to them for other purposes. Pilate used this money to build the aqueduct. But when it was built, because it also served the temple, the Jews protested that a system built with tainted money could not serve a holy place. They gathered below Pilate's porch and rioted again. The encounter turned bloody when some of Pilate's men attacked the Jews and many were killed. Again, Pilate was reported to Tiberius and was publicly reprimanded.

Tiberius decided to come to Jerusalem to see what was going on. Being a good company man, when Pilate learned that Tiberius was coming, he ordered that golden shields be made which would be inscribed with "Hail Tiberius the Emperor." When Tiberius arrived, Pilate's soldiers displayed the shields. To the Jews, this was another case of blatant emperor worship and they rioted against Pilate for the 3$^{rd}$ time. Tiberius ordered the shields melted down and Pilate was once more publicly reprimanded.

Anyone who has ever worked in a large image conscious bureaucracy has got to feel a little empathy for Pilate. Pilate could not do anything right at this point. He was in serious trouble with Rome, but he has not yet figured out why. I once heard a man at Summit Ministries in Colorado tell of an episode that had happened to him when he was part of the war room staff when Reagan was President. He told of being in a crisis mode that required him and his staff to remain at the Pentagon for over 24 hours. By the time he got home, he was exhausted. He said, "I went over and sat down on the bed and took off my socks. I walked into the bathroom with the intention of throwing my socks into the dirty clothes hamper and then making use of the facilities. Instead, I walked over to the toilet, lifted the lid and threw my socks in. I just stood there looking at my floating socks. I knew something was wrong, but I couldn't figure out what it was."

I rather think Pilate was like that. He knew something was wrong, but he didn't know what it was. I think it must have been a day when he was tired. A day when he wondered when the camel would arrive with the last straw. It was a day when Pilate was beaten up. He needed to keep his head down. He needed to avoid any more bad press and, above all, he must not have any more confrontations with the Jews. Yes, I think it was probably a day just like that. Been there, done that and I can see it all. When he'd had just about all he could take, his secretary rings the intercom and tells Pilate that the camel is in the lobby. The Sanhedrin has just shown up with Jesus.

*John 18:29 So Pilate came out to them and asked, "What charges are you bringing against this man?"*
*John 18:30 "If he were not a criminal," they replied, "we would not have handed him over to you."*
*John 18:31 Pilate said, "Take him yourselves and judge him by your own law." "But we have no right to execute anyone," the Jews objected.*

"Execution?" Pilate must have thought. "That's pretty stiff. I wonder how such an unimpressive looking person could have stirred them up to such a degree." Pilate decides to try to talk with Jesus.

*John 18:35 "Am I a Jew?" Pilate replied. "It was your people and your chief priests who handed you over to me. What is it you have done?"*

After debating with Jesus about the meaning of truth, Pilate can see that there are no real charges being brought against, what to him, appeared to be a poor misguided, itinerant preacher who had a God complex. Pilate mutters something to Jesus about truth and goes back out to the Chief Priests and elders. *John 18:38 "What is truth?" Pilate asked. With this he went out again to the Jews and said, "I find no basis for a charge against him."*

As Porky Pig would have said if he had been in charge, "And that's all, folks." Porky would have been right. That should have been the end of the story. But of course, it was not. If you are in a position of power or leadership, I hope you will pay close attention and learn something from Pilate's errors. Bad decision-making pays compound interest. Pilate's past failures had so compromised him with the Jews, that he no longer had any semblance of moral authority. He could not dispose of a simple matter of false accusation. Pilate looked at his choices, the devil or the deep blue sea, and knew he had to do something to appease the Sanhedrin and try to make this thing go away before he himself broke Roman law.

*John 19:1   Then Pilate took Jesus and had him flogged.*
*John 19:2   The soldiers twisted together a crown of thorns and put it on his head. They clothed him in a purple robe*
*John 19:3   and went up to him again and again, saying, "Hail, king of the Jews!" And they struck him in the face.*
*John 19:4   Once more Pilate came out and said to the Jews, "Look, I am bringing him out to you to let you know that I find no basis for a charge against him."*
*John 19:5   When Jesus came out wearing the crown of thorns and the purple robe, Pilate said to them, "Here is the man!"*
*John 19:6   As soon as the chief priests and their officials saw him, they shouted, "Crucify! Crucify!" But Pilate answered, "You take him and crucify him. As for me, I find no basis for a charge against him."*

Did you notice that the story takes an important twist here? Until this point, the Sanhedrin had accused Jesus of being a criminal because they knew very well that Pilate would not, could not get involved in a religious dispute of any sort. Rome prohibited that. But now, in their desperation, the truth comes out.

*John 19:7 The Jews insisted, "We have a law, and according to that law he must die, because he claimed to be the Son of God."*
*John 19:8 When Pilate heard this, he was even more afraid,*
*John 19:9 and he went back inside the palace. "Where do you come from?" he asked Jesus, but Jesus gave him no answer*

Why was Pilate afraid? I think it was because he instinctively knew the stakes he was dealing with. Powerful people get to be powerful people because they have good instincts about what things are really important. I believe that by this time, Pilate knew the truth that Jesus was much more than a man. I believe that because Pilate did what very few have ever done. He spoke up close and personal with the sovereign God of the Universe. No person who ever did that remained unchanged. There could be no other reason for Pilate's many attempts to free Jesus. Why should Pilate care what happened to one more Jew? I think that perhaps Pilate knew that he had come to the crossroads of his life. Jesus left him no way out. Pilate had to side, against Jesus, with the people who could bring about his political destruction. Or side with Jesus against the majority force. The

99

Bible tells us what he did, but history tells us why. Why did Pilate really crucify Jesus? He did it to keep his job.

Could I have laid low and let all of this pass? Was it really necessary to risk everything by insisting on being publicly identified with Jesus? Did I bring this all on myself? No, yes, and maybe. It didn't help at all that many of my Christian friends thought I had done the wrong thing. While there was still time for me to refuse to speak at the Holy Spirit Conference and make amends with Gannett, several of them came to see me to tell me that I was making a mistake. They argued that it was better to have a silent Christian in a powerful media position than to have no Christian there at all. Many of them told me that this could not possibly be God's will for my life. He would not lead me to such a high place and then demand that I leave it over something as silly as teaching a Bible class. I wondered if they were right. But I knew that they were not. God was teaching me something that I had to learn, but I could not adequately explain to anyone at the time. Perhaps I can now.

*Mat 16:21   From that time on Jesus began to explain to his disciples that he must go to Jerusalem and suffer many things at the hands of the elders, chief priests and teachers of the law, and that he must be killed and on the third day be raised to life.*
*Mat 16:22   Peter took him aside and began to rebuke him. "Never, Lord!" he said. "This shall never happen to you!"*
*Mat 16:23   Jesus turned and said to Peter, "Get behind me, Satan! You are a stumbling block to me; you do not have in mind the things of God, but the things of men."*

The Holy Spirit led me to these verses when I entertained the thought that maybe my friends were right. I found it interesting that these verses follow Peter's declaration that Jesus is the Son of God and Jesus is so excited that He immediately made Peter the Pope. But, Peter went from Pope to Satan in 5 short minutes. Fame is fleeting is it not? Jesus knew what His friends could not begin to perceive. He was on His way to the cross. So was I.

Am I suggesting that I suffered anything like what Jesus suffered? Of course not. I'm only pointing out that Jesus could have avoided the cross and still kept His reputation, but He did not. He made it clear that anyone who truly would follow after Him would also face a cross. *Mat 16:24 Then Jesus said to his disciples, "If anyone would come after me, he must deny himself and take up his cross and follow me."* No one made Jesus go to the Cross. He went to the cross out of obedience because that was what His Father required of Him. There is always a choice in the cross. I knew that I could say "not now" to the cross that appeared in my life. My friends would have all understood and most would have agreed that I had made the more prudent decision. But I knew differently.

*Mat 16:25 For whoever wants to save his life will lose it, but whoever loses his life for me will find it. Mat 16:26 What good will it be for a man if he gains the whole world, yet forfeits his soul? Or what can a man give in exchange for his soul?*

Was that really what was at stake for me? Yes, I believed that it was. I was a teacher of the

Word of God. I knew what that meant. *James 3:1 Not many of you should presume to be teachers, my brothers, because you know that we who teach will be judged more strictly.* The truth is that I feared God more than I feared man. None-the-less, it was the most miserable time of my life. I was disappointed with God for what this had cost me. Why had this happened? And why hadn't He rescued me?

*******

I only know how to do one thing when I am lost. I turned to scripture for answers. I began to read about Elijah. Elijah stepped out in faith, put his whole career on the line with the prophets of Baal, by doing this great thing for God's reputation, only to run down the mountain right into the wrath of Jezebel who promised to kill him by the next day.

Did Elijah fall on his knees and thank God for another challenge in life? He did nothing of the kind. *1 Ki 19:3 Elijah was afraid and ran for his life. When he came to Beersheba in Judah, he left his servant there,*
*1 Ki 19:4 while he himself went a day's journey into the desert. He came to a broom tree, sat down under it and prayed that he might die. "I have had enough, LORD," he said. "Take my life; I am no better than my ancestors."*

This great prophet of God, the one who could call down fire from Heaven, was so scared and disappointed that he quit the ministry. He ran off across the desert of Beersheba and hid in a cave. And then the Lord came to Elijah. *1 Ki 19:9 There he went into a cave and spent the night. And the word of the LORD came to him: "What are you doing here, Elijah?"* As I read the passage, I knew that the Lord had never had any sensitivity training. He wasn't nearly as sympathetic to Elijah as I thought He should have been. Elijah is a nervous wreck and all the Lord can say is "Elijah, what are you doing in here? Get back out there and get to work."

*1 Ki 19:10 He replied, "I have been very zealous for the LORD God Almighty. The Israelites have rejected your covenant, broken down your altars, and put your prophets to death with the sword. I am the only one left, and now they are trying to kill me too."*

Elijah said, "Look, I've had enough. I quit. These people you care so much about have broken down your altars and killed all your prophets. I'm the only friend you've got left and they're trying to kill me. And are you grateful? Get somebody else." And I thought, "You go, Elijah." That's just how I feel. I'm done speaking out for the Lord. I quit.

The friends I had left began telling me of the great way God was going to use this in my life. Someone actually suggested that I become a consultant to professional people who are struggling with faith issues. And I thought; "Well now there's an idea. Let's think that through a moment...hmmm. You know I don't know that my example of public humiliation and unemployment is going to be all that appealing to somebody who still has a job."

So, I found myself a cave (actually it was my basement) and I announced to the Lord that I had retired from His public service. From now on He could find me on the back row at church

103

minding my own business. Then I went down to the basement and sat in a rocking chair contemplating my future, or what was left of it. What else was I qualified to do? Nothing. Being the President of a television station prepares you for nothing else in life. I looked at the size of my basement and wondered if I could turn it into a day care center. I could probably manage that.

Then the Lord spoke to me. I knew it was the Lord because, after reading Elijah, I knew that anyone else would have indulged me a little self-pity. He said something like *"Linda, what are you doing down here in the basement? Get out there and back to work."* And I informed the Lord that apparently He hadn't noticed that because of Him, the tabloid press had convinced most people that I was deranged. I checked. My phone wasn't out of order. It just wasn't ringing with job offers.

Well, I suppose in all honesty, I did get one phone call. In fact, it was a really odd thing that happened. Less than a week after I resigned my position, I was contacted again by Dr. Vaagenes. He told me an interesting story of a foundation that had about a million dollars in cash that had been set aside for 10 years to invest in a Christian television station. He asked me if I knew that KTMA, a bankrupt independent television station in the Twin Cities, was for sale. Of course, I knew that. But I could hardly believe that he was actually suggesting that Larry and I should partner together with the foundation and buy it. Larry, who by the way also had a background in television, and I could manage it and live happily ever after. All the foundation members wanted was agreement that the station would provide broadcast access for the Christian community.

I was appreciative of the offer, but I knew a million dollars wasn't enough to buy any kind of television station in a major market. Besides that, no matter what he said, it sounded like *religious* television to me. I knew that wasn't ever going to work and besides, I had already told God that I wasn't doing Him any more favors.

Dr. Vaagenes and the other men on the board, Pastor Alan Langstaff and Jerry Peltier, a retired executive with 3M, assured me that they really wanted a mainstream television station. They wanted a real media outlet that was not hostile to Christian ideals. Further, they wanted it to be profitable because they did not like the idea of living on donations. I was very skeptical. The thing was in bankruptcy now. It wasn't profitable when it was a regular television station. I couldn't see anything that was going to change that. And besides, we did not have enough money. We would have to raise at least two or three million more in a matter of weeks to buy a station that nobody who really knew anything about television would even want. Surely, they did not think I could raise that kind of money.

I had only been in Minnesota for two years and I didn't know that many people and I didn't know any with real money. If I did know any, they weren't likely to give it to me. But having nothing better to do at the time, Larry and I agreed to give it a look. Rich Runbeck, a long time friend and CPA for the foundation helped us to put in place a private placement memorandum. The minimum investment was $40,000. To buy the station, we needed 40 people to invest at that level. I read the memorandum and the description of the property we were trying to acquire and tried neither to laugh nor cry at how it actually looked on paper in the full light of day. It was not pretty.

Channel 23, KTMA, had been in bankruptcy for two years. In its volatile history, it had been a pay-per-view soft porn station, an independent, and now was an infomercial station. Its main revenue source came from psychic lines and sex lines. Although it was licensed to full power, it operated at 25% of its legal capacity due to a severely disadvantaged antenna and delivery system. After the initial purchase price of 3.5 million dollars, it would require another 3 million to achieve parity with the other six television stations in the market. And we really expected 40 people, who had been smart enough to have $40,000 lying around, to invest in that? What were we thinking?

The patron saint of the Twin Cities was Rose Totino. Rose was 78 years old when I met her. I went home one afternoon to find that Rose, whom I did not know at the time, had called and left a message with my daughter Kirsten. I still have the envelope that Kirsten wrote the message on: "Rose Totino wants to invest $5,000 in your company." A phone number was included. I thought to myself, "What an encouragement, unfortunately, I will have to call this lovely lady and tell her that we cannot accept an investment that low." I did call Rose and we talked for about half an hour. She asked me if I had received her message. I said that I had and that was the purpose of my call. "Rose, it's about the amount you want to invest." "Is something wrong?" Rose asked. "Isn't $500,000 enough?"

My lip was bleeding from smashing it into the telephone receiver when I fell off my office chair onto the floor. Later, Kirsten and I had a mother/daughter talk about how to take telephone messages and how to write the correct number of zeroes.

Even with Rose's call, I still didn't see how it could possibly be done. Then the Lord spoke to me again. "Linda, you've raised a million and a half dollars and you haven't left the basement yet." · I knew I needed advice. I decided to give the Lord another chance. I asked Him if there was any possibility that there might really be a plan in all of this. Had He really intended for me to leave my lofty perch at KARE 11 to take on a joke of a television station that nobody who could get a real job would even consider? And at the risk of sounding like one of those people you see wandering around the downtown area talking to the no-parking signs, I believe the Lord said "yes." But I still wasn't sure. After all, I knew people who were convinced that God does not understand thermonuclear energy, so maybe He didn't understand broadcasting either.

I decided to ask somebody else and I called my mentor of many years, Bill Moll, who was by now the President of WNBC in New York. I said, "Bill, perhaps you've heard that I've left KARE." And he said, "Linda, the whole world of television has heard that you left KARE." And I said, "Well, let me bounce this crazy idea off of you. Larry and I are thinking about becoming partners with three men we barely know. None of them has the first idea about how television works, but together we're going to raise a couple of million dollars and buy a bankrupt independent station with a disadvantaged signal, no equipment and no programming, in a market that is already over served by two powerhouse independents. We don't have any money and nobody really wants to work there. So how do you think this would affect my career?" And he said "Linda, how did this happen to you? Did you lose your mind a little at a time or did you just wake up one morning and it was gone?"

And after asking career advice from a number of people, all of whom by the way said the same thing, I decided to ignore it all and give God a chance to show me that He really did understand television. More than that, to show me that He could be trusted.

As I write these words 10 years later, I realize how childish my understanding of God really was and how patient and kind He is when we are petulant brats. Today I shudder to think how brazen it was to think that I was giving God a chance to show me something.

# Chapter 5

## Desperate Times, Desperate Actions

In the romanticized version of this story which some have told, I left KARE, walked across the street and purchased channel 23 out of bankruptcy and made it all look easy. It wasn't quite like that.

In fact, if I had known in advance how difficult it was going to be to actually get a purchase agreement for the station, I don't know that I would have had the emotional energy to go forward. There is a reason why the Lord only shows us one day at a time. When He call us to an adventure with Him, if we really knew what was ahead of us, most of us would never get out of the gate. He insists on one step at a time when most of us want to sprint to the end. As Dutch Sheets has said, "we are into micro waving while the Lord is into marinating."

We did have 1.5 million in hand, but that still was not enough. We had a target deadline with the secured creditors of February 15, 1992 to close the deal and a drop dead date of March 1st with the FCC, at which time our license and right to acquire the station would expire.

This is the point where Bob Beale entered my life. Bob Beale was, and is, the kind of individual about whom no one has benign feelings. Either a person understands him completely and can find a linking thread of genius through his complex view of life, or one labels him an extremist. Bob was a multi-millionaire when I met him and he is that many times over today. I, therefore, fall into the camp with those who say that he is an eccentric genius. Bob, unfortunately, did not always enjoy the wide berth of public tolerance offered to other complex people, who are often pardoned for their irregular views because their contribution to society is so apparent. Bob's contribution was sometimes difficult for mere mortals to grasp and he often said of himself that people had a tendency to misunderstand him. If you asked Bob what he did for a living, he would tell you that he was a rocket scientist. In fact, that is precisely what he was.

Although Bob was widely recognized for his scientific acumen, what often made him the topic of water cooler conversation was that he was believer-in-God to the $10^{th}$ power. His view of faith was part prophetic, part positive profession, and uniquely his own. I remember the day he explained to me how tall God is. That question never once crossed my mind, but if you've always wondered about God's height, according to Bob, God is just over 5'9". We were in a business meeting once with a group of young managers who worked for Bob in his computer business. Bob asked the group at large whether or not they could see the angels that were in the room. I couldn't see any myself but maybe they did because they got very quiet after that.

Bob imagined how things ought to be and then proceeded toward them as if they were really that way. In some ways, he was a visionary. There is no doubt that we would not have proceeded and acquired channel 23 had it not been for Bob's actions and participation.

Beginning with John Santikos years earlier, the Lord had trained me to work with and to have an appreciation for people who provided their own drum beat for life. I have been privileged to know many complex and even difficult people in my life, to whom I have had a variety of reactions. It has been my observation that people who are truly genius or gifted in some way often have trouble negotiating through relationships with other people. I actually considered myself to be quite good at dealing with these kinds of people because my years in television had required me to manage many stars and stars' egos. Bob Beale, however, is the only person I've ever dealt with who has driven me to physical violence. Actually, it was just short of physical violence. I've decided that it serves no purpose to elaborate here on the incident itself, let it just be said that in the middle of one of our endless meetings, I sprang out of my chair like a piece of toast, climbed across the conference table determined to sock him in the nose before my attorney intervened. I realized then that if I didn't get a grip on the fact that Bob saw the world differently from me and just about everyone I had ever known, that our inability to speak the same language would drive me to the brink of insanity. At that time in my life, it would have been a short trip.

We met Bob for the first time at Rich Runbeck's office on October 31, 1991. I remember it well because it was the day of the Great Halloween snowstorm. Bob listened to Larry and me explain our ideas for how a "Christian-friendly" television station would work. We then told him that we still needed to raise 2 million dollars to close the deal and would be looking for additional investors. Bob smiled and said "look no more" and that he would purchase all the remaining shares. The entire meeting took about 30 minutes. I was beginning to think that either there was nothing to this capital raising business or I had missed my true calling in life. At this rate, we would have the whole thing wrapped up in 30 days, surprising the most skeptical of the onlookers. I ignored my intuition and experience that told me that anything that looks too good to be true, usually is.

I realize now that I was merely naïve and idealistic. I honestly assumed that if a person said that he would invest 2 million dollars in a project, that quite naturally, that meant that he *had* 2 million dollars. Silly me. When Bob told me that he did not have that kind of cash in a checking account, but would have the money soon, I wasn't worried. It sounded logical to me that a person with the enormous assets that he was known to have, would quite naturally have to rearrange them for a major investment.

Confident that the deal was done, Larry and .I went to the National Association of Television Programming Executives (NATPE) in New Orleans to begin buying the programming we needed for channel 23. Because Bob would be the senior partner in the deal, we invited him and his wife Becky to go with us, which they did. I knew that it would take all the capital that we could raise to close the deal on the station. That meant that we didn't have any actual cash to buy programming. But we went on the assumption that because I had over 25 years experience in television and had managed 3 stations before, and that Larry was also well known in syndication circles (even before his debut on Entertainment Tonight), that our contacts in the business would allow us to structure pay out deals. Further, in addition to the secured creditors of the television station, there was another million dollars in unsecured debt owed to the major program distributors. If they had any hope of being paid back, the station had to be operating. I figured that our chances of painting that kind of picture to the creditors, people who already knew us, were pretty good.

I remember in living color sitting in the foyer of the New Orleans Convention Center in January, when Bob Beale told us that things were not progressing for him as he had hoped and that he was not going to be able to close the station deal after all. The closing date was 2 weeks away and the most he could come up with was $500,000. But, we should not worry because he felt that something would turn up and we would be able to close the deal anyway. I hate optimists. Especially when they are optimistic about something about which I am sure that they know absolutely nothing. I felt like we were wasting our time and even misleading people with whom Larry and I had worked for years by trying to buy programming without any real money for a station that we did not have and seemed unlikely to get. It was very humiliating and I just wanted to go home.

Bob felt that we should go ahead and keep all of our appointments at NATPE as if everything were going to work out just fine. I felt like an imposter. Perhaps it is my arrogance showing, or perhaps it is my experience showing, but there are two things that really annoy me: people who waste my time and people who cannot be trusted in financial matters. Therefore, my number one rule for business etiquette is that I have tried very hard not to waste the time of other people. I did not want to waste the time of people I had known for years by implying that I was in a position to do business when I was not.

Regarding financial matters, I was and still am of the opinion that one of the most unfortunate witnesses in Christianity today is the poor regard in which people of faith are often held by the secular world when it comes to finances. As a group, we have proven over and over that either we don't really understand how business works, or we can't be trusted. In television, of the many organizations that buy "time," meaning commercials or programs, from Sushi knives to "Abs of Steel," there are two categories who must pay in advance: politicians and tele-evangelists. Some ministries are notorious for getting themselves into debt with no plans whatsoever for getting out. How many envelopes have you received this month with "crisis" or "emergency need" stamped on the outside? I receive one or two a week. Always from a ministry who is serving the Lord and going bankrupt at the same time. Perhaps I don't get it, but I simply don't believe that the Lord has somehow gotten Himself into a cash crunch in half the ministries in America. Neither do I believe that the reason so many ministries are in this condition is that the devil is attacking their good work. Please. Not only are these "crisis," "emergency," "we're going down the drain" appeals disingenuous, but also they sound silly and irresponsible to anyone who has ever had to balance a checkbook.

I wasn't about to intentionally join the ranks of people for whom I had so little respect. If I couldn't see the plan to pay for the obligations I might incur, I would not incur them. No doubt this strong conviction I had was instilled in me in those years when my family had lived in such self-imposed poverty. Be that as it may, it was also the reason that very large corporations had trusted me to manage very large sums of money. In order to go ahead with the programming deals with people whose professional respect I hoped to retain, I would have had to imply that I actually had a television station and operating capital. At this point, that didn't seem likely to occur. Home, James.

Then Bob Beale said something to me that rang as truth in my consciousness. He said that I could not possibly know what the Lord might do that would allow us to go forward and to close the deal by the deadline. True. He went on to say that what I did know was that the window to purchase the programming that we must have to begin operations should the Lord do something, was right then. Also, true. He said something like this: "You must do *now* the things that can be done *right now*. You cannot do *now* the things that are 30 days down the road. Do what you can do today, the Lord will take care of tomorrow."

Thinking back, I'm not so sure that what he said was all that profound. But it worked for me because it caused me to break character and go forward in structuring the deals when I could not clearly see how it was going to work out. I was up-front with the distributors that this deal still had a few bugs to work out, but I was confident about the outcome. We agreed to put in place a fail-safe clause for them in case the station deal did not close. They were not at risk. I, on the other hand, wondered about the damage it would do to my resume and my personal reputation if everything went south, which was the direction we were currently pointed. Anyone will let you waste their time once, but in business, you don't get three strikes before you are out.

Over the next two weeks, we met with any number of potential investors. None of whom could see the wisdom of investing in a widow maker television station that no one in 13 years had been able to make profitable.

By February 13<sup>th</sup> at 5 PM, we had not raised any more money. I sat in my basement and tried to figure out what to do when the Lord spoke to me again. In fact, He told me precisely what to do. I must confess that I didn't think much of His idea. The Lord told me to break ranks and bypass all 10 lawyers involved in this case and go straight to the bankruptcy trustee with a different proposal that would allow us to close by the March 1 deadline. I did not want to do this for two reasons. Reason number one is that I believed that the lawyers knew more about such things than I did and that if I followed the Lord's instructions and it didn't work out, that everyone would be madder at me than I was sure they already were. The second reason that I didn't want to do it was because the Lord's idea could not possibly work. I believed that the Lord had told me to take the money I had and ask the trustee to take the 1.5 million we had in the bank, close the deal on time and "trust us for the rest." Right. "Lord," I said, "if that could work, don't you think that these high dollar lawyers of mine would have thought of it? It is too simplistic. How can that possibly help?" Then the Lord reminded me of someone else who once thought that the Lord's ideas were too simple.

*2 Ki 5:1 Now Naaman was commander of the army of the king of Aram. He was a great man in the sight of his master and highly regarded, because through him the LORD had given victory to Aram. He was a valiant soldier, but he had leprosy.*

Bummer. Here is a military officer who has everything going for him. He is successful and highly regarded by the people and his king. He has probably never been sick a day in his life. Suddenly, he is stricken with an illness that could not be kept secret. It was very visible. Further, it carried with it the shame associated with diseases like AIDS. Those who contracted leprosy were not just sick. They were unclean. They must have misbehaved in some way. Naaman's wife had a servant girl who had been taken captive from Israel. The servant girl loved her mistress and wanted to help.

*2 Ki 5:3 She said to her mistress, "If only my master would see the prophet who is in Samaria! He would cure him of his leprosy."*

You know there are any number of ways that Naaman's wife could have responded to the servant girl. She could have rebuked her for saying anything at all. She could have said, "Thank you very much, dear, but where did you say that you got your medical training? I see. Thanks and all that but I believe that we will just stay with more orthodox medical treatment." But she did not. Instead she told Naaman about the prophet.

Even more amazing to me is the fact that Naaman listened to his wife and asked the King of Aram for permission to go and find the prophet. The king was not only delighted to send Naaman to get help, but wrote a letter of commendation for him to the King of Israel. Eventually, Elisha the prophet learns that Naaman is on his way to the King and he sends a message to the king instructing him to deploy Naaman to the prophet's home.

*2 Ki 5:9   So Naaman went with his horses and chariots and stopped at the door of Elisha's house.*

Naaman knew how to make an entrance. No doubt Naaman thought that once Elisha realized how important he was, that the prophet would pull out all the stops to see that Naaman got priority handling. But it did not work. Elisha was unimpressed. In fact, he might have even been annoyed at such a display of worldly power. Whatever the reason, Elisha did not bother going to the door himself. He sent his servant.

*2 Ki 5:10   Elisha sent a messenger to say to him, "Go, wash yourself seven times in the Jordan, and your flesh will be restored and you will be cleansed."* Take two aspirins and call me in the morning. Was Naaman impressed? Not exactly. *2 Ki 5:11   But Naaman went away angry and said, "I thought that he would surely come out to me and stand and call on the name of the LORD his God, wave his hand over the spot and cure me of my leprosy.*
*2 Ki 5:12   Are not Abana and Pharpar, the rivers of Damascus, better than any of the waters of Israel? Couldn't I wash in them and be cleansed?" So he turned and went off in a rage.*

I suspect that Naaman had turned his horse around and was headed for home. But then the story takes an interesting turn. One of Naaman's lieutenants took him aside and encouraged him to look at things another way.

*2 Ki 5:13 Naaman's servants went to him and said, "My father, if the prophet had told you to do some great thing, would you not have done it?*

Those words virtually leapt off the page for me. The Lord's instructions to us are seldom complex. We are the ones who insist upon complexity. The Lord was saying to me, "Linda, if I had told you to do some difficult thing, would you not have done it? Obey me and do this simple thing." I knew the Lord had a point, but first I wanted to know what had happened to Naaman.

*2Ki 5:14 So he went down and dipped himself in the Jordan seven times, as the man of God had told him, and his flesh was restored and became clean like that of a young boy.*

"Ok, Lord, I'll give it a go." The trustee was a man named Don Johnson, revered as the premier bankruptcy attorney in the Twin Cities. I was not supposed to talk to him directly. Only the attorneys who were on my side were supposed to do that. But, the Lord had specifically told *me* to call Don Johnson up and offer him a different deal.

I had every intention of obeying. I had the phone in my hand, but then I faltered. I hadn't gotten over being a corporate soldier yet. A corporate soldier does not arbitrarily go stepping over the heads of the $200 per hour attorneys and their $40,000 worth of now worthless documents to do his own deal. I tried to tell the Lord that if I did it His way, the attorneys would quit and I didn't have any money to hire any new ones. I felt that the better way to go was for me to talk to my own attorneys and make them realize that desperate times call for desperate actions. I was sure that, although they had as much as said the deal was dead, I could convince them that I had heard from the Lord and they should call Don Johnson one more time on my behalf and explain the Lord's ideas to them. So, I called my half of the 10 lawyers and told them that I had a new idea for a different deal. The Lord was right, of course. They thought it was ridiculous and that no one would go for it and they refused to present it to the other side. After that, I called Don Johnson.

He did not respond with great enthusiasm, but he did not hang up either. He said that he would think it over and call me back later that night. He did call and we were to meet at 9 AM the next morning with the lawyers from the opposing side.

Now would be a good time to tell you about Miles Kennedy. Although Miles eventually came to work for us at channel 23 as the controller, at the time he worked for Rich Runbeck and had been assigned to help me with the acquisition of channel 23. I've tried many times to describe Miles to other people. He is the most non-threatening person I have ever met. Sometimes when I use that word to describe Miles, others wonder if it is a dubious compliment. It is not at all. If you are a person in business, as I tell you more about Miles, you will gain a new appreciation for having someone on your side who could be the poster boy for the Boy Scouts. He was honest, kind, truthful, helpful, and an eternal optimist. I know what I said earlier about optimists, but by now I had sort of warmed up to the idea of having one around.

Miles and I have been through many tumultuous times together when things looked pretty bleak. At least they looked bleak to me. The worst they ever looked to Miles was "not too bad." In fact, I am not sure that Miles has ever had a bad day. If he had a spiritual gift par excellence, it was that he was an encourager. My husband, Larry is an encourager, too, but even he paid homage to Miles' incredible ability to expect everything to work out just fine. For example, when we finally got the station, our cash flow was so tenuous that we tracked our revenue every day. When I would ask Miles how the numbers were looking, he would always say, "Not too bad, things are looking up." That is how I knew when to duck. "Things are looking up" was Miles' way of saying that "we've got bombs on the left and bombs on the right and the main engine just fell off."

Miles and I went together into the arena at the offices of Briggs and Morgan, the lawyers for the creditors, on February 15th. All 10 attorneys stood around the table snarling like hungry lions. My attorneys were still annoyed with me for calling Don Johnson directly so they were behaving like spurned lovers offering me no emotional encouragement at all. The bankruptcy attorneys for the other side weren't all that happy about it either. The ten of them lined up around the wall looking as if they hadn't eaten anyone in months and Miles and I were the catch of the day. It was brutal.

They accused us of reneging on the original deal. They accused us of intentionally misleading them and creating thousands of dollars of extra work. They accused us of being underhanded and dishonest. They accused us of trying to steal the station. If it hadn't been so serious, I would have almost felt complimented. We were not nearly clever enough to be guilty of all the schemes they accused us of conjuring up. The attorneys for the creditors hadn't really liked the deal very much when they thought we had 3 million dollars. They really didn't like it now. They said my idea wouldn't work and that their clients would not accept it. Don Johnson called for a recess. The flogging was scheduled to resume in 20 minutes. During that 20 minutes, Miles wandered into Don's office.

If Miles had not chosen a career as a CPA, he could have worked for government intelligence. Miles is so disarming that people will tell him anything. In that 20 minutes, Miles learned that the only other serious contender for the station (whom we believed to be right outside the door with a certified check in hand) had in fact, folded his tent and gone home when it seemed certain that we were getting the deal. In other words, time was running out and we were the only players left at the table. Our chances improved immediately.

On February 29$^{th}$, we closed the sale of channel 23. If it had not been leap year, we would not have made the drop-dead date of March 1$^{st}$ when our right to the license would expire. It had been a long battle for our side. I realize that to onlookers, the fact that it only took 6 months from the day I left KARE until we owned our own station, does not seem like a very long time. But it was every hour of every day of 6 months.

On the morning of February 29$^{th}$, as I stood in front of the mirror fluffing my hair and smoothing out my green dress which I would wear to the closing, I remember saying a prayer and thanking God for helping us on this journey to the promised land. Then God spoke to me again. "This is not the Promised Land." "You're kidding, what

is it?" said I. "This is your first day in the desert." I
wondered what He meant by that.

# Chapter 6

## Guerilla Brigade

We walked into channel 23 on March 2$^{nd}$, 1992 as the new owners. Sort of. We still owed 2 million dollars to the creditors. The first installment of $200,000 was due in 60 days and the balance within 12 months. I walked into my new office, closed the door behind me and thought, "What was I thinking?" I suddenly realized that I did not have the first idea as to what to do next. Perhaps I ought to start with the program schedule. When you looked up our channel listing in the TV Guide, it mostly read "TBA" which is television talk for "to be announced" or in our case, "we don't have a program right now but hope to get one before anyone notices." The television set has been a part of the American Experiment for so long that most people don't think about what it takes to actually have pictures with sound and motion on the air 7 days a week, 24 hours a day. That is a lot of programming.

More and more, it is common to turn on local stations to find the 30-minute programs known as *infomercials.* These are the programs that convince you that what you're missing in your quest for wealth, beauty and happiness is an investment in ostrich farms; a miracle wrinkle/fat loss pill all in one; or maybe magic magnets to cure whatever ails you. These programs are on the air because their creators pay big bucks for the time to sell their products. Lo, but it is truly amazing what people would rather have than money in their pockets. The programs also fill holes in a program schedule. A shorter version of these programs comes in two-minute segments under the acronym of DR (direct marketing.) I know it should be DM and I don't know why it is not, but trust me, in the trade, we call it DR. The DR versions move things like videos for slice and dice kitchen marvels and, the even more lucrative psychic and sex lines.

When we arrived at channel 23, the station had managed to continue operations because of the infomercial and DR business. More than $400,000 of annual revenue was derived from the sex lines and the psychic lines for our station. Because of our audience size, we likely had the smallest allocation in the market. When one considers that many if not most stations take this business in some form, it is shocking how much money is out there for telephone pornography and fortune telling. Our first week in office, we cancelled all of the sex and psychic business. Half of the remaining sales force quit in protest. If they didn't have sex and psychics to sell, what did we expect them to do? Good question. The sales department did not have a lot of confidence in the programming deals we had made at NATPE. Old movies and a few situation comedy series from the '80's did not excite them.

I was beginning to realize that I was handicapped by the fact that I had never worked for a small company. The two companies that I had worked for had been big and were fully established. They had office buildings and checking accounts with money in them. They had vice-presidents and human resource departments. When I called with a problem someone answered the phone. I never before had to think about where things like operating capital came from. Whether I worked for Gannett or Harte-Hanks, I simply called the home office and told them what I needed and they put the money in my local bank. I felt terribly insufficient when I finally figured out that *I* was the home office in our new company. We had a staff of 40 people and not enough money in the bank to meet the first payroll. In spite of all of our dreams and ideals to be a new kind of television station, out of necessity our focus had to sharpen. I shifted mental gears from idealistic to survival mode. We developed a simple operating motto and pasted it to everyone's desk: "Sell spots, collect money. Happiness is positive cash flow."

It is important to say here that from the first day to the last day we were never delinquent in paying a single vendor, were always able to meet our operating expenses, and we always made payroll. I've been told that our competitors in the market had wagered that we could not operate for more than 90 days. They were very aware of our struggles and could make a pretty good guess as to how much operating capital we had, or did not have as the case was. So how did we do it? We worked as hard as we could, prayed as hard as we could, and the Lord sent us manna. There is no other explanation for it. We had equipment that wouldn't work; a transmitter that wouldn't transmit a signal strong enough to reach the entire coverage area; and programming that no one would watch. It would have been easier to shut the whole thing down, gut the place and start over in 6 months. I couldn't remember why I had thought this was a good idea. Miles, on the other hand, thought that the opportunities were endless.

Shutting down and starting over was not an option. First, because if a station goes "dark" it's license becomes open game for a challenge. Second, we were out of money. The only hope we had of raising the additional 2 million was to be an operating entity. In order to meet the first payment of $200,000, we had to find new investors very soon. In those first few months, my time was divided between trying to find new investors and trying to make channel 23 look like a real television station. It was like working on the engine of a car while it is running. You have to be very careful where you stick the screwdriver.

I was in the lunchroom one day when our newest sales person, Rachel Hagfors, came in with her yogurt. Making small talk and meaning nothing at all, I said to her, "Rachel, don't you have any relatives with money?" I was kidding of course because if Rachel, who was in her 20's, had any connections at all, I was sure that she would not have come to work for us. Her reply was "sometimes my father likes to invest in small companies." That is how I met Norm and Vangie Hagfors.

The day that the Hagfors came to channel 23, I was watching for them out the window of my office. They drove up in an Oldsmobile. Before I met with any new potential investors, I always tried to get a look at their car. I had developed a very scientific formula as to how much risk investors were likely to take based on the kind of car they drove. For example, Bob Beale drove a Jaguar. That meant high-risk tolerance. Rose Totino drove a Cadillac. That meant solid American values and moderate idealism. I figured that Norm and Vangie might be good for $40,000 according to my car formula, but probably no more than that. It was not a perfect formula.

Vangie was very warm and friendly and Norm was an engineer. We went into our small conference room at the station where I tried to convince them that an investment in channel 23 was not nearly as risky as it might look. Norm would ask me questions and I would give the answer. To which Norm never said "good answer or bad answer." He just went on to the next question. When they left, I had no idea what they thought of channel 23. Norm called the next day and said that they would like to invest $200,000 and that he wanted a seat on the board of directors. It wasn't long before I learned that Norm had been one of the original founders of Medtronic and had patented the first pace maker and was probably worth more millions than I would ever be required to count. I tossed my car formula in the trash right after I signed the check to the bankruptcy lawyers, meeting the deadline for the required first payment of $200,000.

That same week, while reading a copy of *Nation's Business*, I saw that the new president of the National Chamber of Commerce was Bill Lurton, CEO of Jostens. I had met Bill Lurton one time when I had been at KARE. I wrote a letter to Bill, reminded him of who I was, told him what I was doing and asked if he would invest in our company. That part about me being who I was did not impress him, but he did have a good sense for business potential. He invested $50,000, which gave us the operating funds we needed to fix some of what was broken and allowed us to remain on the air. Before it was all over, Bill would invest well over $300,000 and also become a board member.

After Bill Lurton, I was fresh out of ideas and contacts. Further, the station was demanding more and more of my energy and time. I was learning an important lesson about size and critical mass. Managing a big station as I had done before is a lot like driving a tank. A tank just rolls along on its own momentum. If anything gets in the way, it either rolls over the top of the obstacle or shoots it. The driver of the tank can stand up and poke his head out of the tank and look around at the scenery without worrying that the tank will get off track. Managing a small station, however, was more like driving a sports car at a high speed. You must keep your hands on the wheel at all times or you end up in the ditch.

One of the most important things that I have learned about God in this adventure, is how precise is His sense of timing. From the first day until the last, there was simply no way that we could have "planned" for things to happen in the sequence that they occurred. The week when reality set in that I was out of prospects for investors, 3M offered an early retirement package to some of their employees. Jerry Peltier accepted the offer and came over to channel 23 to take over the job of finding investment capital.

Not only did Jerry bring every subsequent investor to the table, but he convinced Cush Minar, owner of Minar Ford and one of our first investors, to increase his investment to the $200,000 level and to come on the board. Eventually, Cush would become the largest single shareholder in the company and a fervent prayer warrior. Jerry brought in Chuck Dietz, former chief counsel for 3M, and Carl Kurhmeyer, another former senior executive for 3M. One by one he brought all the rest to the table until we had over 40 investors, reaching our goal and paying off the secured and unsecured creditors. Until I met Jerry, I had never known that deal making was a spiritual gift. Jerry had also been a pilot for 3M. Like my car theory, I had a plane theory. The smaller the plane a person would get in, the greater the risks he was willing to take. Jerry had a high tolerance for risk. I, on the other hand, am right at home in a 747. When I was at the Gannett school of management, I was taught, "when you get into trouble, follow the rules." I tried to do that from time to time at channel 23. Didn't work. There weren't any rules. I tried but I couldn't find the handbook for what we were doing. So whenever things got tense, I had a tendency to regress to corporate protocol. Jerry would remind me that I was no longer a corporate soldier. I was now leading a guerilla brigade. The rules and the risks were different. But, I still had a hard time getting over being corporate.

Our board now consisted of Bob Beale, Alan Langstaff, Jerry Peltier, Carl Kurhmeyer, Chuck Dietz, Bill Lurton, Norm Hagfors, Jerry Peltier, Warren McClean, Craig Roberts, and me. I was the Chairman of the Board. These men were well known in the Twin Cities for their professional achievements. Others often remarked that it was a very prestigious board for such a little bitty company. Some have asked me what it was like to work with such powerful men, each of whom was accustomed to being in charge. Larry said that it must be like being the mediator for presidents of small nations. It was. They took their roles very seriously and had never seen a rubber stamp in their lives.

As a board, we faced many high-risk decisions in moving our company forward. As nearly as I can remember, except for one time, we were always unanimous in our decision making. The question that I am often asked by business writers is, "Was it harder because I was a woman?" No, it was not harder. It was an advantage. If I had been a man, I am not so sure that we could have been as successful in coming together on every issue. Frankly, I don't think that our little company could have handled any more type A testosterone. In fact, even if I had been a very good feminist, I am not certain that we could have worked together so effectively.

I suppose that I should explain what I mean by that. I am a strong advocate for equal opportunity for women and equal pay for equal work and all that, but I dropped out of the "women's movement" long ago. One of the reasons is because the women I saw moving weren't necessarily going anywhere I wanted to go. I had long ago decided that every battle being championed by NOW and others, for me was not only, not worth fighting, but certainly not worth winning. There are issues of equality that I do think are important. My experience is that men and women come up with better ideas and solutions together, than either group does segregated to its own species. That is why I thought it was a good idea when our law firm offered to appoint both a male and a female attorney to our account, a combination I believe is usually the best team in just about any circumstance I can think of. A man and a woman see things differently. Not better or worse, just different. How does it help to have two people with an identical perspective and worldview? Unfortunately, the female attorney attended only one board meeting and never attended any others although she stayed on our team. I suppose that the freewheeling, candid style of our board meetings was just not her cup of tea. It is also probable that the board might have leaned a little too far to the right for her comfort zone. The truth is that I think she really checked out over that Rush Limbaugh/feminnazi discussion, but it's just a guess.

Were these men chauvinists? Not at all. In my mind, they were just about perfect. They were gentlemen. They were brilliant. They were loyal and steadfast. They were honest and honorable. They were devout Christians. They were experienced and unrattled by the normal ups and downs of business. They supported me in the difficult times and they gave me the credit in the good times. They were also demanding and tough minded on the hard issues. They constantly challenged me to improve performance and to grow the business. They were all bottom line thinkers, but so was I so we got along very well. All of these men had all made their fortunes and established their reputations long before a good idea about equality became a hybrid force called militant feminism. They were completely unacquainted with fanatical politically correct speech. So they didn't know that, according to some, I should have been insulted when Cush referred to me as "Queenie" or "Your Highness" and Chuck would inquire if "the princess" were in? At the beginning of every board meeting, they shook hands with each and hugged me before we would sit down to pray. I could never work up to being offended by their genuine display of affection for me. They always treated me with respect and absolute trust. They and their wives and Larry and I had a cherished relationship that I am sure will never be duplicated in my lifetime.

What was the one decision on which we did not have unanimity? In 1994, Alan Quist ran for the office of governor and asked me to be his running mate. I thought it was a good idea and that I could join him in the campaign in addition to running the station. I knew that according to the polls, Mr. Quist was unlikely to win, but I admired the fact that a professed Christian was willing to get into the fight whether or not the odds were on his side. I admire people who go to battle over principle and I wanted to help. My board, on the other hand, was not so sure that we would not win and they told me that their confidence and that of other investors would be shaken if I took on political causes. I declined to run.

The secured and unsecured creditors were finally paid off and we and Richfield Bank now owned the station. But we still had many problems. We had no programming advantage at all. There was nothing about our station that made us unique or "must see TV." Part of the problem was me. Well, OK most of the problem was me. I just could not get a grip on what a Christian friendly television station was supposed to look like. I tried to acquire programming that offended no one. It must have worked because "no one" watched regularly. I learned quickly that what Christians said they would watch on television and what they actually watched was entirely different. Rating book after rating book proved that either Neilsen does not place diaries and meters in Christian homes, or Christians watch television like everyone else.

Was that disappointing to me? Maybe it was, but I can understand why people do what they do. There are just so many battles that an individual can fight. In the typical American middle class young home today, what do we have? Many times we have two working parents and two or more very needy children. Both husband and wife work because so much of the time it is out of necessity. I wish that it were true that every family can make adjustments if they really want to so that one parent can always be home, but it is not always true. Working parents are not cut any slack in the demands of their day jobs simply because they are parents and have additional full time jobs waiting for them when they come home from the office. The demands of home, work, church, extended family, debt, traffic, sometimes illness and all that goes on in life is just about all the stress a mere mortal can handle. When that mother and father come home fully spent of intellectual and emotional energy, they do not get to go out with a drink and sit in the hot tub while nanny and the butler take over. Mommy and daddy get to keep on working. They work on homework, work on the house repairs, work on the lawn, work on the laundry, work on dinner, and work on cleaning up. They are worked out. They cannot take on another cause. At the end of it all, they collapse into the only refuge available to them: the living room sofa. Most of the time, they turn on the television set and they watch whatever makes them laugh or whatever allows them to stop thinking, working and coping for even a short while. They are too tired to swim against the current anymore, so they go along with the flow of the culture that is manifest on television. Unfortunately, the flow always goes downhill.

The point of reckoning for the truth about "Christian" television came for me when I learned that the broadcast contract for the "700 Club" which aired on the Fox affiliate was up for renewal. We contacted Pat Robertson's organization with full confidence that they would be eager to move their program from the "evil empire" owned by Rupert Murdoch to a family friendly station owned by other Christians. They politely declined our offer and renewed with Fox. Their reason? Our appeal was too narrow. We were too "Christian."

Not since the day I tried to sock Bob Beale in the nose had I been so angry. I went into my office and I slammed the door, dropped to my knees and told the Lord that I wasn't leaving until He explained to me what was going on. This was turning out exactly like I had told Him it would. Not even Christians will watch Christian television. And who could blame them? It was boring. I had been obedient. Furthermore, I had convinced all of these good people to invest their hard-earned money into a broken down television station that had more problems than a run-over dog. Why? Because the Lord had said He would help me. I told the Lord that I had done just what He had told me to do and He wasn't doing anything. Fortunately, He did not smite me. He spoke to me instead. But I couldn't believe what I was hearing. He said, "This isn't what I told you to do." Then He led me to a story in scripture that I never knew was there.

*2 Sam 7:1 After the king was settled in his palace and the LORD had given him rest from all his enemies around him,*
*2 Sam 7:2 he said to Nathan the prophet, "Here I am, living in a palace of cedar, while the ark of God remains in a tent."*
*2 Sam 7:3 Nathan replied to the king, "Whatever you have in mind, go ahead and do it, for the LORD is with you."*

*2 Sam 7:4  That night the word of the LORD came to Nathan, saying:*
*2 Sam 7:5  "Go and tell my servant David, 'This is what the LORD says: Are you the one to build me a house to dwell in?*
*2 Sam 7:6  I have not dwelt in a house from the day I brought the Israelites up out of Egypt to this day. I have been moving from place to place with a tent as my dwelling.*
*2 Sam 7:7  Wherever I have moved with all the Israelites, did I ever say to any of their rulers whom I commanded to shepherd my people Israel, "Why have you not built me a house of cedar?"'*
*2 Sam 7:8  "Now then, tell my servant David, 'This is what the LORD Almighty says: I took you from the pasture and from following the flock to be ruler over my people Israel.'"*

I read this passage and the Lord gave me the meaning. David, so grateful to the Lord for what He had done for Him, decided to build the Lord a temple. But the Lord said to David, "I didn't tell you to build me a temple. I told you to be the King of Israel." In that moment, the Lord said to me, "I didn't tell you to build me a temple. I told you to build a television station." That crashing sound was the dawn breaking in my spirit as I finally got it. From that moment, I stopped trying to run channel 23 like it was a church and began operating it like it was a real television station. We would continue to provide access to the Christian community in public affairs or any other venue that seemed reasonable. For example, we produced a Christmas and Easter special with a salvation message for India that ran on the national network and was viewed by over 450 million people each time that it ran. Pastor

Alan Langstaff and I co-hosted a weekly public affairs program entitled "Crossroads." The program dealt with contemporary issues that were in the news from a Christian perspective. "Crossroads" provided a forum for pastors and other ministry leaders in the Twin Cities to participate in the moral debate in the marketplace of ideas. We produced many video pieces for other ministries to use in development or recruitment.

But we also began to acquire programming that would actually attract an audience. We acquired "Matlock," "In the Heat of the Night," "Sightings," and "Hunter." Tame by today's standards, but the kind of programming that Christians we had surveyed said they did not care to watch. But, of course they did and so did others. Our ratings began to grow and we began to make enough money to actually move forward a little.

How do I know that the Christians were watching? I got mail. Identifying themselves as Christians, some people wrote chastising letters to me to let me know how disappointed they were that the programs they never watched were no longer on the air. My son, Chris, attended Bethel College at the time. One of his professors said to him, "I'm really disappointed that your mother took all of the Christian television programs off the air." "Really," Chris replied, "which ones did you watch?" His teacher answered, "Actually, I never really had time to watch any of them." "Then you won't miss them," Chris replied.

The fact is that I did not take all the Christian programs off the air. Our entire morning lineup Monday through Friday consisted of Christian teaching or preaching ministry programs. We finally became secular enough so that the "700

138

Club" moved to our station. It was actually very popular with a daytime audience. But the program that was the most popular and that Christians, conservatives, and each of my board members insisted remain at any cost was the syndicated "Rush Limbaugh Television Show." We had the broadcast rights and it aired at 9 PM every night.

I realize that most people have no reason to know how program syndication works. In order for you to understand how an enigma of huge proportions can develop, I need to explain the nature of the syndication beast. One syndication, or production company, may own, produce, and distribute the broadcast rights to a number of programs that do not appear to be connected to one another at all, but really are. Just as Colgate may make different toothpaste's and shampoos under different names; or just as Estee Lauder markets cosmetics under that name and under the name Aveda and others; or one conglomerate owns several department store chains; so one syndication company may own many television programs that, to the public, seem unrelated. Much to the utter amazement of my board, the program distributor for "The Rush Limbaugh Television Show" was the same distributor for "Sally Jesse Raphael," and "The Jerry Springer Show." In 1993, Norm and Vangie Hagfors and Jerry and Darlene Peltier attended the NATPE program conference in Miami with Larry and me. It was a rhema moment for them when we walked into a cocktail party hosted by MultiMedia Inc. where Phil Donahue, Jerry Springer, Rush Limbaugh and Sally Jesse Raphael were all present, accounted for and laughing it up with each other and the television executives who came to buy their shows.

It isn't enough that a station may want to buy a certain syndicated program. The programs go out on a bid basis, but they do not necessarily go to the highest bidder. If that were always the case, channel 23 could never have had any programs because we could not outbid anybody. Very often, one syndication company will own the rights to a "hot" program that everyone wants and will also own a couple of bow-wows that nobody wants. In order to get clearance for the lesser program, syndicators use their leverage by placing the hot program a station does want on its channel, only if the station will also take the doggie program that it doesn't want and put that program on the air as well.

That is how it came to be that in order to retain the rights to "The Rush Limbaugh Television Show," we also had to take "The Jerry Springer Show." Unlike other markets, we were the first to refuse to put the Springer show on in the daytime. We put it on the schedule at 11 PM, far out of reach of children. It became the highest rated program on the station. I had a love/hate relationship with Jerry Springer. I loved the ratings and the revenue it generated, but I hated the fact that it was on channel 23. We monitored the program every day and refused to run many episodes due to content. We kept a generic episode to plug in when the daily dose of Jerry was just too vile. The producers would wail and threaten me whenever this happened. I blamed it on engineering and lamented about how hard it was to get good help. But there was only so far that we could go before we were in violation of the contract. If I took the program off the air completely, not only would we lose the revenue, but we would also lose the "Rush

Limbaugh" program, for which there was no forgiveness. This was another one of those decisions I had grown to dread. Again, I had to choose between something bad and something worse. If I kept Jerry Springer, the Christians would demonize me with no possibility of explaining my decision. But If I lost Rush Limbaugh, I was dead. Ecclesiastes 9:4 reads *"Anyone who is among the living has hope --even a live dog is better off than a dead lion!"* I opted for the live dog part and renewed the Springer show.

# Chapter 7

## Fish in Dark Water

It was December of 1994 and we were having our monthly prayer meeting in the studio. I was thinking about Jerry Springer and how much I wished that I didn't have to air that program on channel 23. Suddenly the Lord spoke to me again. But before He said anything, He brought to my mind a vivid recollection of an insignificant incident that had happened the summer before.

In Minnesota, we all do the same thing for recreation. We go "up north." When my son Chris was first invited by some of his friends to go "up north," he came home, looked at the map, and asked how much further "up north" one could possibly go? Going "up north" means that you are going to the woods and the lakes where you will camp out or go to your cabin depending upon your economic status in life.

Larry and I had had outgrown camping out and couldn't afford a cabin, so we compromised and bought a camper trailer and parked it on a lot that we had leased near Hayward, Wisconsin. A dozen or so other couples had done the same thing, so we had a small trailer community on Spider Lake. We had the mandatory lawn chairs and camping stuff scattered around our trailers. A friend of ours visited us from the cities and said that our camp looked like a K Mart sidewalk sale. That was the summer that I decided to learn how to fish. Many people in Minnesota and Wisconsin plan life around fishing season "up north." There are two fishing seasons up north: summer when reasonable people fish and winter when the radical participate in what is known as ice fishing. And that is precisely what it is. When the lakes are frozen to 20 inches, little tin and cardboard ghettos spring up like mushrooms in the middle of the lakes of Minnesota and Wisconsin. Inside are otherwise normal looking men who cut holes in the ice with a chainsaw, sit for hours on little fold up aluminum seats, and fish. They do not freeze because they have little kerosene heaters in their ice houses to keep them warm. Yes, you have read this correctly. In the middle of a frozen lake, they place heaters on the ice. Heaters that put out heat. Heat that melts ice. They will sit there for hours and sometimes days waiting for a fish to swim by. I have known people who have given up the sport of ice fishing when they got saved and stopped drinking hard liquor. One man explained to me that since he quit drinking, he had noticed that sitting on the ice in twenty degrees below zero weather with a string in the water was not really all that much fun. Every year, there are several accidents on the lake when one of the pick up trucks that had been driven out there (how did you think they got to the middle of the lake?) would crash through the ice and someone would be seriously hurt or even die. I promised my children that although I did not know how my life would end, I could promise them that it would not be as a result of driving a vehicle atop a frozen lake to fish. The idea of sitting in the sun on a clear lake and catching fresh fish for dinner in the summertime however, was very appealing to me and, besides, I needed a hobby. So Larry and I bought a pontoon boat and went shopping for fishing gear.

Our boat was white with aqua trim. I thought it would be nice to buy fishing gear in complimentary accent colors. Larry didn't know any more about fishing than I did, so he let me pick out what I liked. We bought all kinds of lures and bobbles in shimmery corals and pinks with just a hint of turquoise. Then we took Kahlua and drove our boat out to the middle of the lake where the sun shone the brightest and dropped our lures in the water. We could work on our tans while waiting for the fish to bite. For the first hour, I practiced casting and Kahlua practiced barking. He was so excited. He had never been fishing before and he couldn't decide whether he was supposed to jump in the water and go after the lure or just bark at it. He opted for barking since he hadn't ever been swimming in a cold lake before either.

I wasn't sure what the point in casting was anyway. Was the fish supposed to chase the lure and jump on it like a cat chases a paper wad when you throw it? Or was the lure supposed to hook the fish? However it was supposed to work, it wasn't. So I decided to just let it bob there in the water with one of those little cork things. Which, by the way, are not made out of cork so I don't know why they call it that. Larry was already napping when I leaned my head back and closed my eyes. Kahlua was asleep on the swim deck. The sun was warm, the sky was blue, God was in Heaven and it was just like I had imagined it would be. Well, I had not actually imagined that Kahlua would turn over and roll off the edge of the boat into the 75-degree water, but he did.

He started barking and I was yelling for Larry to wake up. I grabbed my fishing rod and reeled in the line so that Kahlua wouldn't get caught up in it. Then I thought that maybe I could slip the end of it under his collar and hold him up while

Larry pulled him back in the boat. Of course, I realize now that it was a stupid idea, but at the time, I wasn't sure. Anyway, while I was poking at him with the end of the rod, Kahlua thought I was hitting at him so he got scared and started swimming in circles. In his panic, he swam under the boat where we could not reach him. I told Larry that he was going to have to jump in, swim under the boat and get the dog out. Larry told me that Kahlua weighed 40 pounds *before* he got all that long fur sopping wet and that he was not going to die from hypothermia and leave me a widow from trying to save a brain-damaged dog. Larry then laid down on the boat and hung his head off the end so that he could see underneath where Kahlua was hiding out.

In just a minute or so he was able to coax Kahlua out from under the boat so that we could grab his collar and drag him on board. I'm pretty sure that is why we didn't catch any fish that day. What kind of fish would hang around a drowning dog and a screaming woman? Made perfect sense to me.

We waited a long time just to be sure that all the fish had left, caught nothing and went back to the camp. We were tying up the boat where Wally, our neighbor, was cleaning his fish on the dock. As we walked by, Wally cast a wary look at Kahlua, who still had that deer-in-the-headlights look in his eyes. Wally asked, "What were you doing out there?" "Fishing," I replied. I mean, wasn't it obvious? "You won't catch any fish out there in the sun," Wally said. "You have to fish along the shores, in the shadows, where the dead trees are." I knew where he meant of course. He was talking about those swampy looking inlets scattered around the lake. Where the dead trees stuck up out of the water making it very tricky to try to get a pontoon boat in there. The trees that weren't dead hung down making it dark and yucky looking and it smelled like mildew and dead fish. Thanks, but I'll just wait out there in the sunlight until a fish swims by. It's bound to happen.

And so we waited. Nothing. Larry got tired of waiting for fish that weren't coming and took up reading instead. After a week of this, my tan was coming along nicely but we were still not catching any fish. We came back to the dock late one afternoon and there was Wally, cleaning more fish than I was sure was allowable. I walked over to him and said that maybe I would try fishing in the dark places he had mentioned. He peered over his horned rimmed glasses at my color coordinated lure, pole, hat and fishing outfit; then to my manicured nails and diamond tennis bracelet and fluffy dog. (I had used a hair dryer to blow dry Kahlua's fur and he was looking especially nice that day.) Wally looked skeptical. "What are you planning to use for bait?" he asked. "Oh, I think I'll just stick to these nice lures that I bought in town," I said swinging a particularly spiffy looking one. "Won't work," he said without looking up again. "What do you use, Wally?" "Leeches," he said and pointed to a bucket filled with pulsating slime. "If you want to catch fish in this lake," Wally said, "you have to use smelly bait and fish in dark water." He had to be kidding. I wouldn't even want to catch a fish that would eat one of those things.

I decided that a compromise was in order. Larry drove me out in the boat to the edge of the dark water so that I could sit in the sun and still cast my line and designer lure into the swamp. Days went by but no fish ever did. For all of our investment in fishing tackle and a boat, we had nothing to show for it and the summer was going fast. Larry did not care and neither did Kahlua, but I was now desperate to catch a fish. So I went over to Wally's trailer and said, "OK, I'll try it. Where do I buy leeches?" "Too late," Wally answered, "leeches are out of season."

As I sat in the studio that afternoon in December for the prayer meeting, the vision that came to my mind was Wally. He was standing there saying to me "If you want to catch fish, you have to use smelly bait and fish in dark water." Then the Lord spoke. He asked me what I thought the people were like who stayed up late at night to watch programs like the "Jerry Springer Show?" I thought to myself that they must be people who couldn't sleep and had nowhere to go. Maybe they were people who were looking for lives that were more desperate than their own. Maybe they were people who didn't have any friends. Then it came to me. Clear as a sterling spoon on Waterford crystal. "Need a friend? Call this number." I saw it plainly. Crawled across the bottom of the screen on "The Jerry Springer Show" at 10 minutes intervals were those words.

Two of our prayer partners and faithful friends were Dan and Diane Morstad who ran a crisis counseling phone center called "Love Lines." I asked Dan what he thought about putting the Love Lines phone number on the screen during the Jerry Springer show with the "Need a friend?" message and seeing what would happen. He agreed to try it. None of us could have predicted what did happen.

From the very first night, callers overwhelmed the crisis counselors. Yes, some of them were pranks, but the great majority of the callers were the very kinds of people that the Lord had shown me were out there. They were lost, alone, depressed, and desperate to talk to someone who might pretend to care about them. When the people called in, they were given whatever help they needed. Many of them, literally *thousands,* were led to the saving grace of Jesus Christ over the phone and sent for follow-up to local churches. We continued running this message in Jerry Springer for the next 4 years. Every night was a repeat performance of the night before. As the ratings for the program grew, the number of calls increased. Additional telephone lines and staff were needed.

Dan Morstad said that from the first month, they realized that the entire nature of their ministry must change. Until the Jerry Springer experiment, most of the people who called the ministry were already Christians or had some experience in the faith. Not until the calls started coming in from "The Jerry Springer Show" did the counselors realize that they had never really talked to the truly lost people of the world. They were accustomed to calls from people who had some sort of spiritual need and wanted someone to pray with them. They were not trained for the call from the gay male stripper who was on the verge of suicide because his lover had left him. They were not trained for the gang member who had just witnessed a beating. The telephone counselors had to have new training and learn a new vocabulary. Younger counselors from the local colleges were recruited. Jerry Springer may have been the most effective evangelist in the Twin Cities.

But not everyone appreciated our attempts at evangelism. Some still criticized the fact that we had the "Jerry Springer Show" on the air even when they knew about the "Need a friend?" line. I prayed a lot about this. "Lord, I thought, if this is of you, why am I still criticized for it? Isn't there something else I could do instead?" And I believe that the Lord said, "Yes, you can go sit in your boat in the sunshine and hope that a lost person swims by. Or you can keep fishing where the lost really are."

Does what happened with Jerry Springer mean that trash talk shows have a redeeming value or that somehow this exonerates me from the responsibility of having such a program on the air? No, it does not. What it does mean is that in a fallen world, sometimes, the only pieces we have to work with are broken pieces. Life is not neat and tidy. It means that in the midst of no alternatives except bad alternatives, God can and does fish for the lost. He still goes where too many of us in the faith refuse to. He goes go into the dark places after His lost children and He woos them to come to Him.

Even non-Christians know about Jesus' friendship with prostitutes and social reprobates. We marvel at the willingness of Jesus to socialize with such misfits. But what about the misfits? Why did they hang out with Jesus? What was it about Jesus that made them want to be with Him and to trust Him? How did He get invited to their houses? There are still plenty of prostitutes and reprobates around, not to mention tax collectors. Why aren't they having Christian leaders over for wine, dinner and a little conversation?

They probably would invite some of us to come, but I feel rather sure that many of us in the faith today would not go. We have our reputations to think about. How would it look to go to the house of a pagan for beer and barbecue? We would be too afraid that the deacon might think we were too worldly if we are seen leaving the house of a winebibber.

George Barna sent a wake up call to the American church in his startling book <u>The Second Coming of the Church</u>. Barna's dispassionate research irrefutably proves that the American church is having no impact whatsoever on the culture we claim to disdain. Most church growth comes from people leaving one church to go to another. There is practically no true evangelism taking place among churchless people. Why? We have a problem in the church today that prevents us from reaching really lost people. We act as though we are convinced that we are very different from them. We are willing to admit that we are not perfect and that we are sinners, too. But we don't really mean it. We are convinced that their sins are real sins and that ours are just weaknesses. We know that maybe we eat too much, but gluttony isn't really as bad as drunkenness. Maybe we don't tithe all of the time, but the Lord overlooks it because we're so good in other areas. Maybe we did cheat some on our taxes, but we've never stolen anything from a real person. We look at the male stripper who called in from "The Jerry Springer Show" and think "at least I'm not like him." Jesus told a story about that kind of spiritual arrogance.

*Luke 18:10 "Two men went up to the temple to pray, one a Pharisee and the other a tax collector.*
*Luke 18:11 The Pharisee stood up and prayed about himself: 'God, I thank you that I am not like*

*other men--robbers, evildoers, adulterers--or even like this tax collector.*
*Luke 18:12 I fast twice a week and give a tenth of all I get.'*
*Luke 18:13 "But the tax collector stood at a distance. He would not even look up to heaven, but beat his breast and said, 'God, have mercy on me, a sinner.'*
*Luke 18:14 "I tell you that this man, rather than the other, went home justified before God.*

Why did the prostitute, the tax collector, and the leper run toward Jesus when they run away from modern Christians? I believe that more than anything else, the world is looking for authenticity. Lost people are desperately looking for found people who really care about them, but they are not finding them in the church. Far too often what they find are plastic people awash in spiritual pride. What does that mean? Kris Kristofferson once wrote these lines: "Everybody's got to have somebody to look down on. Who they can feel better than at any time they choose. Someone doing something dirty decent folks can frown on." Is that how we look to the lost? Is our self righteousness showing?

Do I think that God really had anything to do with causing "The Jerry Springer Show" to be on our station? I don't know that He *caused* it. But I do know that God will work with whatever we give Him. *Rom 8:28 And we know that in all things God works for the good of those who love him, who have been called according to his purpose.* I think that "all things" means "all things." I would much rather have had the Billy Graham Television Crusades as part of my legacy, but I did not get an opportunity to choose Billy Graham. I chose "Rush" and got Jerry in the bargain. But Jerry brought some very nice fish into the kingdom.

# Chapter 8

## Saved by the Wind

When we arrived at channel 23, the audience was not suffering from poor television or inadequate service. Because the Twin Cities is a major market, the quality of local television was among the best in the country. In terms of the competitive opportunity for a new station, the market was fully mature. Minneapolis/St. Paul is the 13$^{th}$ largest television market in the country. It is served by all seven television networks, a public television station and a fully wired cable market. The viewers were not waiting for us to rescue them from lack of choice. Choice was all over the place. The nature of the competitive environment made it very difficult for an undercapitalized new station, like us, to get into the game at all. At this point we were not trying to beat anyone in the ratings race, we just wanted to play.

Perhaps I can contrast the competitive challenge we faced in 1992 with the hot start Internet world of today. In contrast to broadcast television, which is a mature business, the Internet dot COM world of the new millennium is still in its startup friendly era. Anyone with a good idea can still find a niche to serve on the net. Even with little capital, it is relatively easy to start an Internet business because the industry is so new that even the longest term players are still immature and the audience, or their consumer base, has not had time to develop loyalty to any one service. The consumer is therefore willing to try any new flash and dash that comes along. Not so in television. Most Americans develop station preferences while they are children, and unless they move to a new city, they stay with their favorites. If a new station comes to town, even if it offers something better, the viewers are reluctant to try the new channel out until and unless their station of choice gives them a reason to shop around.

In other words, it isn't enough in a mature competitive environment to have a new source of programming. The new station cannot make real progress against its closest competitor until that competitor makes a mistake or has a franchise that it is willing to give up. Television station franchises are things like being "the news station," or "the comedy station," or "the sports station," or the "kids station." It is very expensive to attain dominance in any of these franchises and dominance is expensive to defend once attained. For channel 23 to make headway in an overcrowded television marketplace, our closest competitor had to make a tactical error and we had to be ready to seize the moment when and if it happened. It happened for us in 1995 when the Fox affiliate, owned by Nationwide, was sold to Clear Channel Communications.

WCCO, the CBS network owned and operated (O&O) station in the market, owned the sports franchise of the Minnesota Twins baseball team. Being the home station of the Twins meant that WCCO was required to broadcast a majority of the games. This is difficult for an "O&O" to do because of the station's first obligation to carry all network programs without pre-emption. Therefore, in order for WCCO to fulfill its obligation to the Twins, it had to have a partner station that had the flexibility to carry all of the games that conflicted with the WCCO's network coverage. The Fox station had been WCCO's partner in the Twins baseball franchise for a number of years. When Clear Channel came to town, Dan Sullivan was the President of the Television Group and John Culliton was the Vice-president and General Manager of WCCO.

I was not present at the meeting between Sullivan and Culliton when the terms of the Twins partnership were discussed, but I have had business negotiations with both men. Therefore I know something about the personalities involved. Culliton was young, smart, corporate, a gentleman, a favorite son of the Midwest and a rising star in CBS. Sullivan, on the other hand, was a gunslinger. I use that characterization because Dan Sullivan often described himself in similar terms. The first time I met him, he dropped by for a visit to tell me that our station looked and felt like a Clear Channel station. He then informed me that he would be buying us out of channel 23, and that we had better all get used to the idea that "There is a new sheriff in town." The fact that channel 23 was not for sale did not seem to dampen his bravado. I knew that the meeting between Culliton and Sullivan was going to happen and I secretly wondered how Minnesota nice and Rambo were going to get along.

I didn't have long to wait. I figure that their meeting had been over for about 45 seconds when John Culliton called me on his cell phone as he pulled out of the driveway of the Fox station parking lot. He wanted to know if channel 23 had any interest in being partners with WCCO in the Twins franchise if they decided not to renew with the Fox station. "Gee, I don't know, John, we've got all these great 'I Love Lucy' episodes to air." I don't know when I have been so excited. This could be the break we had been waiting for. There was this one little problem, however. Remember when I said that we had a transmitter that couldn't deliver a signal to the entire coverage area? That was still the case when the Twins opportunity appeared. My guess is that the reason Sullivan took such a hard line position with Culliton was because he assumed that there was nowhere else for WCCO to go with its games. After all, the Twins would never agree to have their games transmitted on a station that couldn't quite reach the city limits.

John wanted to know if we had any plans to address the tower and transmission problems we were having. I told them that I was working on that very item and could give him an answer in a week as to when we could be up to full power. The fact is that while I had been very concerned about the problem, I had not been working very hard on it because it was difficult to motivate shareholders to raise another 1.5 million just so that everyone in the woods outside of town could get a clear picture of Lucy and Ethyl. But now that we might get something like the Twins that was different. If you have ever worked in a large company, perhaps you can imagine the stacks of paperwork and the endless meetings that would have to take place to get such a large capital request through the approval process. It takes months, not a week.

I was beginning to see the advantage to being "the home office." We could move quickly. We could make decisions without going through layers and layers of corporate gobblety gook. We called a shareholder meeting, told them about the opportunity and asked for permission to sell enough additional stock to raise 1.5 million dollars for a new transmitter, antenna, and to upgrade our production facility. Slam, dunk, the vote was done and Jerry Peltier hit the streets to sell the new shares, which sold as if we were actually making a profit. Existing shareholders bought most of the shares, but several new people who had been on the sidelines came in also. Construction began almost immediately on the antenna work at the tower.

Some observers have trivialized our insistence that the success of channel 23 was as a result of the Lord's continuous watching over us. Most people who hold to that point of view have difficulty in understanding that the Lord does not make the distinctions between the secular and the ecclesiastical as some of us are prone to do. Does God get involved in the affairs of the "real world?" Yes, He does. He owns it after all. Some have maintained that given the experience that Larry had in television and cable and marketing, and my years in television, with a little luck and good timing, anyone could have done the same thing. Maybe so, but before reaching that conclusion, let me tell you about the day we had the accident at the tower. It was during the installation of the new antennae.

The broadcast tower is in Shoreview and rises 1500 feet in the air. It is the tower for the antennae of three television stations and 12 FM stations. The antennae for the television stations are closer to the top of the tower and all of the FM's are lined up below. The radiation factor is so high near the top that in order for any station to do any work, the rest of the stations must agree to "power down" to enable the technicians to work in such a high "RF" environment. The day that channel 23 was to do its antennae work was on a Saturday.

Larry was painting the deck and I was helping him by keeping Kahlua out of the paint and pointing out the spots he missed when the phone started ringing around noon. There were hysterical calls from the general managers of most of the FM stations telling me that there had been an accident at the tower that had very nearly knocked all of the radio in the Twin Cities off the air; not to mention putting lives and property in danger. I went to the station immediately to meet with Steve Lunde, the chief engineer at channel 23. Here is the story as he told it to me.

The engineers were raising a 20-foot piece of steel weighing several hundred pounds to the place near the top where our antenna was positioned. A cable snapped, causing them to drop the beam and it fell to the ground. Not only were there 12 FM antennae under us, but also there were also three small buildings at the bottom of the tower where the transmitter personnel worked. Next to that was the parking lot that was filled with the employee's cars. I could feel the color leaving my face as I asked him about the damage and whether there were any casualties? Dreading the answer, I asked how many of the FM antennae we had knocked off since a beam of that weight would have fallen strait down and sheered them like a razor. He had to tell me twice before I could process his words. The beam had not hit any of the antennae on the way down. "But how is that possible?" I asked, relieved but not believing that I was getting the straight story. Steve replied, "The wind blew the beam away from the antennae." Suddenly, I was angry. How strong would the wind have to be to blow a steel beam of several hundred pounds off its downward course? Why were we working in an environment where there was that much wind? What were we thinking to put men 1500 feet in the air during that kind of wind?  Steve looked me in the eye and replied, "There was no wind."

I don't like it when people play word games or want to play "20 Questions" when we are dealing with serious matters.   Steve was an engineer. Engineers don't usually try to be clever and Steve was no exception.   "Steve, tell me again exactly what happened."   "The cable snapped and we dropped a 20 foot beam.  Although it had been a calm day up until that point, the wind suddenly gusted out of nowhere and lifted the beam so that it moved to the right and landed on a grassy knoll about 50 feet away from the closest structure.  It hit nothing on the way down.  It hit nothing on the ground.   There was no damage or injury of any kind."

"First, you tell me there is no wind," I said, "Then you tell me a wind powerful enough to move hundreds of pounds of steel 50 feet away just suddenly blew up and dropped the beam where it could do no damage.  How do you expect anybody to believe that story?"  Steve was strangely calm when he replied; "I am telling you the wind did it. You may come to a different conclusion about what moved the beam, but that is my story and I'm sticking to it."

We have often talked about what could have happened that day. First of all, it is a miracle that no one was hurt or killed.   Beyond the horror of a possible tragedy, if the beam had hit even one antenna and knocked another station off the air, the lawsuits would have so overwhelmed a small company like ours that it is very doubtful that we could have recovered.  Could a gust of wind really have moved so heavy an object already in a free fall? I do not know. But, that's the official story and we're sticking to it.

In less than 3 months, we finished all the tower work and went from being the broken down station that no one could tune in, to having the best signal in the market and the only completely digital editing suite in the Midwest.

The new technical capability enabled us to get yet another important sports franchise: the Minnesota Timberwolves basketball team. After that, we became partners with the WB network and became the "kids station" in the afternoon. We expanded our partnership with WCCO and co-broadcast the 10 PM news on both channels. Both stations carried the same main block of news, after which each channel had different stories and the viewers could select from a menu of choices. We were rolling, having fun, making news and we began making money.

We were a real television station now and sales and marketing had become the main emphasis of our operation. Larry oversaw the promotion and production departments along with Wendy Kocon Sedlachek and Todd Ziegler. Most of Larry's time was now needed in developing marketing programs and packages for the sales department along with Dave Petersen, who was the General Sales Manager. My job as the President of Lakeland Television (channel 23) was to keep my eyes on the horizon. Larry, Dave and Miles were in charge of silver linings. I was in charge of watching for the clouds that usually come with them. None of our board of directors or any of our shareholders had any experience in television, and therefore, had no basis to know what kinds of clouds to watch for. By 1997, I could see that things were about to change dramatically in the broadcasting environment. The rewrite of the Communications Act in 1994 was now beginning to make its impact felt. The big media companies were now allowed to get much bigger and were buying up small independently held companies at a rapid pace.

It is helpful to understand the quandary that single station owners found themselves in, if you first understand a little more about how programming is sold. There is what is known as the "one to a market" rule. That means that when we bought "The Rush Limbaugh Television Show" for the Twin Cities, no one else in the market could buy it or air it. It is called "exclusivity" and is fundamental to television. With the buy-up of small groups of stations and independent operators, program deals were quickly being done in New York for whole sections of the country rather than on a market-by-market basis as had been common when there were many owners of television stations. For the syndication sector, it made sense to make one deal with one owner of 20 stations than to fly in and out of individual markets to see how much the little guys would pay. We were no longer getting the opportunity to bid for programming.

I told my board that we had to come to grips with the fact that if we were going to operate in the best interests of the shareholders, we must consider whether or not the time had come to sell channel 23. Prices were at a premium and unless we could find an alternative way to grow our franchise, we would be remiss in not considering the inevitable. The board agreed. But how much was channel 23 worth?

The typical way of valuing a television station is a certain factor times cash flow. That might have been the method we would have used and it was certainly the method recommended to us by the investment bankers that we hired to help us. That would have made channel 23 worth between 25 and 30 million dollars. I felt it was worth more, but I did not have an argument to persuade anyone, although Jerry and Miles agreed with me. Some of the other board members thought that I was too emotionally tied to the station and couldn't make an impartial determination of its worth. There were many interested buyers in the 25-35 million-price range. The board was looking to me to give them a reason to hold out for more. I could not come up with a single thing. I asked the Lord to help me, but apparently, He wasn't talking to me right then.

Then one night, I had this really amazing dream. I dreamed that Rupert Murdoch, media mogul par excellence and head of the Fox Empire, came to visit me in my office. Although Mr. Murdoch had been to the Twin Cities in the prior year, he had not stopped by for tea at channel 23. I had never met the man. Yet, here he was in my dream, standing in front of my desk like we were real chums and he told me that channel 23 was worth 50 million dollars, and not to sell for a penny less. In my dream, I said to him, "Is that gross or net? Thank you, I'll tell my board right away."

At the end of the week, we were scheduled to meet again with Dain Bosworth, the investment firm representing us, to haggle and hopefully agree on the price we would accept for the station. I said that I believed that channel 23 was worth 50 million dollars and that we should not accept a penny less than that. The lead banker said to me, "But, Mrs. Brook, *why* do you think that? What do you base that on?" Without my nose growing a single inch, I said, "Rupert Murdoch told me." Everyone was very impressed. Channel 23 went on the market for 50 million dollars, net to the shareholders."

I've thought about that dream many times since. I know that the Lord speaks to people through dreams, although I don't know that it had ever happened to me. People who know this story have asked me if I thought it really was the Lord who spoke to me and if it was the Lord, why didn't He just say "Linda, this is the Lord speaking. Channel 23 is worth 50 million dollars. Over and out." Why would the Lord speak to me as Rupert Murdoch? First, I am sure it was the Lord. And I think that He spoke to me as Rupert Murdoch because the Lord speaks to us through images in dreams and terms that we can understand. One cannot read Genesis 37-40 without marveling at the dreams and interpretations through which the Lord brought Joseph to freedom and saved Egypt from famine. Moreover, the Lord knew what I did not. He knew that there was a window to maximize the value of channel 23 because the federal regulations were to change again. The Lord knew the timetable and what was needed to move us forward. If I had gone into a room full of lawyers and investment bankers, and told them that the Lord had spoken to me in a dream and told me that the station was worth 50 million dollars, the next sound to be heard would have been the slamming shut of six highly polished brief cases as they all headed for the nearest door. What I needed was an "expert" opinion. So the Lord gave me exactly what I needed exactly when I needed it.

After we set our price tag, we had many lookers and tire kickers who were interested in buying channel 23. All of them thought it was over priced. When the prospective purchasers would present us with an offer that was below the $50 million net, we would decline. They would then proceed to tell us what the station was worth to them. They always came prepared with elaborate charts and graphs to prove how generous their offer was. Then I would tell them that Rupert Murdoch had told me that channel 23 was worth 50 Million and that would pretty much end the discussion. Very few people are really prepared to argue with the success of the Murdoch Empire.

On May 13th, 1998, 7 years from the time I left KARE television, we sold channel 23 to Sinclair Broadcasting for 52.5 million dollars, which netted 50 million dollars even to the shareholders. When one does the math and remembers the 3.5 million dollars we paid for the station to start with, the profit return to investors was 1600% on investment. Many people who had invested their retirement money with us became wealthy. Those who were already wealthy became much more so. Out of the proceeds of the sale, almost two million dollars went back into the Christian ministries and colleges of the Twin Cities as a tithe. North Heights Lutheran Church alone received almost $800,000.

There was one other incident concerning the tower that may or may not mean anything, but is certainly worth noting. On May 13th, Miles and I sat at Richfield Bank and began signing the checks to distribute the $50 million to the shareholders. It was a day when I understood the meaning of complete redemption. All Christians understand the redemption from sin. We take for granted that we will get to Heaven. But far too often we do not expect that God will intervene in this life and redeem the here and now. I had asked God to restore me in the presence of my enemies as He had promised to do in Psalm 23. And He did. Those who had laughed at us stopped laughing. The business magazine, "City Business" put us on the front page and said that my words were now viewed as golden in the investment community. It wasn't my words at all. It was the words of God that I had stood on for 7 years. On the 14th of May, we watched on-line as the bank account with the shareholders' money was drawn to zero as everyone cashed their checks. On May 15th, a tornado struck the tower at Shoreview knocking our antenna to the ground. Channel 23 was officially off the air for several hours until a backup system could be triggered. There was a definite break, even a time of darkness, between the ownership of Lakeland and the ownership of Sinclair. Was there a spiritual message in that? Some think so. Sinclair's policy concerning the Christian community and ministerial programs was quite different from that of Lakeland and most of their access was denied. Sinclair discontinued the "Need a friend?" message in Jerry Springer as soon as they discovered it was there. Todd Ziegler remained at the station for a time after Lakeland departed. He said to me one day, "When Lakeland left, the Holy Spirit left also."

From the tenuous beginning until the victorious finale, the Lord had told Larry and me the same thing: there would be a first day and a last day to channel 23 and He would be in charge of every day in between. I have not mentioned before that one of the ways that the Lord kept us on track and encouraged was through a man named Harold Eatmon. Harold is a prophet in Twin Cities. Perhaps some would be reluctant to confess that many of their key decisions were made after hearing a prophetic word. Larry and I were not reluctant. We believed that the Lord was involved in the events of channel 23 from the beginning until the end. We considered it a gift that the Lord not only spoke to us but confirmed His words through one of his prophets, not once but many times. Harold encouraged us when things looked bad and reminded us that what appeared to be natural events, in fact had serious spiritual value. Harold told us early in the process that the Lord had revealed to him that our lives would forever be divided between "life before" and "life after" channel 23. And it appears that he was right.

# Chapter 9

## Run Towards the Roar

After the sale of the station became public, it was pointed out to me by a reporter that many people before Lakeland Television had tried to make a success of channel 23 and had failed. What made the difference for us? That is a very good question. It is also the reason why I wrote this book. We were a very small group of people who all said "yes" to an adventure with the Lord. Prior to channel 23, we were mostly unknown to one another, but we became much more than a company. We became a family in the Lord. The Lord had said that if we would follow Him, He would lead us across a desert to the Promised Land. He did exactly what He said He would do. There were many points along the way when we could have crashed and burned, but we didn't. Once when another communications company attempted to make a hostile bid to the shareholders, but failed completely, the Lord showed me a scripture that I knew was for us:

*Psa 105:12 When they were but few in number, few indeed, and strangers in it,*
*Psa 105:13 they wandered from nation to nation, from one kingdom to another.*
*Psa 105:14 He allowed no one to oppress them; for their sake he rebuked kings:*
*Psa 105:15 "Do not touch my anointed ones; do my prophets no harm."*

Were we supernaturally protected? Absolutely. My attorneys warned me in the beginning that 85% of companies that are bought out of bankruptcy are back in bankruptcy in less than 3 years. How could we possibly expect to beat the odds?

Another reporter who had been following my personal story from the time I left KARE asked a different question. How does a rather ordinary small town girl from West Texas go from a successful career in television to abject humiliation and despair, and then on to wealth, restoration, and victory in such a relatively short period of time? A very respected leader in the faith called me and said to me, "You know Linda, it doesn't always happen like this. There are many martyrs who never saw their reward while still on this earth. Have you thought about how unusual your circumstance is?"

If I hadn't thought about it before, I began to think about it then. Had this adventure ended as it had because we were smarter than others who have ventured out with the Lord? I seriously doubt that. Why was there such a clear beginning, middle and end to this chapter of my life? I think I know the answer and it is the reason that I am desperate to tell it to others who are about to be summoned to the crossroads of their lives. It is about choice. Let me try to explain. Many times Christians arrive at a crossroads. That means they must decide to go one way or the other. They cannot choose to stay where they are. They must make a choice. When we get there, we pray something like this: "Oh, Lord, please close the door you don't want me to walk through. Force me to go your way." At the risk of offending some, not only is this an immature way to pray, and while it may work for baby Christians for a while, once we reach a level of maturity in the Lord, it won't work anymore. The Lord is about to do the most significant work of human history on this earth. He is calling forth Gideon's army to accomplish that. He is looking for the 300 who can drink water from their cupped hands while looking about for the enemy at the same time. That means He is not only looking for willingness to go to battle, He is looking for fitness to go to battle. The Lord brings us to the crossroads of our lives and insists that we make the decision as to which way we will go. He will not make it for us. He is not interested in taking away our free will. If we choose to go with Him, we will be responsible for that decision. We will not be allowed to blame the Lord for doing something to us. I believe that the Lord blessed my journey from the crossroads of my life as He did, not only because of my decision to follow Him, but because He is desperate to show others that He can be trusted.

*Jeremiah 29:11 (KJV)*
*11 For I know the thoughts that I think toward you, saith the LORD, thoughts of peace, and not of evil, to give you an expected end.*

Did you get that? The Lord thinks good thoughts about us and desires to give us the expectations we have for our lives. But we must trust Him when He calls us. God is moving all over the world right now. He is calling some of us to go with Him. But we cannot have it both ways. We cannot stay where we are and go with God at the same time.

I recently spoke at a Women of God conference where someone asked me to talk about the discrimination that I had faced as a woman and as a Christian. I am pretty certain that I disappointed the person with my answer. I said that the thing for which I am famous in the Twin Cities had nothing whatsoever to do with discrimination or what someone else "did" to me. The devil has no authority to do anything to me. It was the Lord Himself who brought me to the point of decision. My story is about choice and free will. It is about the moment when the Lord takes us up on "I'll go where you want me to go" and all that. It is a story about growing up in our walk with the Lord and our fitness for the battle that is ahead. And more than that, it is about the provision of the Lord for those who are willing to step on a wild ride with Him.

The sovereign Lord of this universe understands what He has created and He orders the footsteps of the righteous. Not because we have any righteousness of our own, but because we are clothed and armored by the blood of Jesus Christ. The Lord knows how to redeem His own. Not because we are faithful, but because He is faithful. Not because we are good, but because He is good. Not because we make every right decision, but because He covers our mistakes and makes them work anyway. Do all things work for good for those who love the Lord? No, they do not. In fact, to translate that verse in such a way as to suggest that we can pile up bad thing after bad thing and that it will somehow make something good is blatantly unbelievable. What the verse does say is "In all things, God works for the good of those who love Him and are called according to His purpose." In all things God worked in my life from the day I made my decision to leave KARE until the present. He worked in the good and He worked in the bad. He worked in the right decisions and he worked in the wrong decisions. I did the best I knew how, but that was not nearly good enough. I was not smart enough, righteous enough, or experienced enough. But God was enough. God can and will do amazing things with obedience.

It hardly seems that it has been 10 years since I came to the crossroads of my life and left KARE in what looked and felt like total defeat. This is also a good time to point out that when such a career crisis occurs, it is not uncommon for the person involved to lose not only his or her reputation along with losing position, but many times the person's marriage is also a casualty. When I decided to leave my very lucrative position at KARE for the great economic unknown, Larry never once reminded me that the reason we were in Minnesota to start with was because he had been willing to leave his job to pursue my job. He never suggested that I think it over and do the math. If the circumstances had been reversed and he had been the one to toss his career out the window because he had heard from the Lord, I am quite sure that I would have been up all night, coming up with all kinds of reasons why common sense should prevail. I would have given him a Valium. I would have insisted that he take some time off and think about it. I would have been very persuasive that the Lord didn't really mean for him to put his family at such risk. Whether or not those thoughts ever crossed his mind, he never said. Not only had he been willing to allow me to be the "show horse" while he was the "work horse," but he stood by in total support when many of our friends thought he should tell me to get a grip.

Being completely on the other side of the events that marked the crossroads of our lives, I would like to tell you what I think it all meant.

Every Christian, I believe, at some point in life will reach a crisis of faith. Sometimes it may be public; most of the time it is not, but it is never the less, a crossroads in the person's life. However one chooses to respond, life is not going to be the same as it was before. While we might feel as though we might die from the stress, few of us actually do. Those of us who don't die try to find a way to make sense of what has happened. We all get *to* the crisis but we don't all get *through* the crisis. By God's grace, we got through ours.

Why do I want some of you to know my story? Because I've learned that no matter how things are for you today, your life can change in minutes. At some point, "Life happens" to everyone. It is crucial that the men and women, whom God is raising up for the end time army, be able to discern how God is involved in what appears to be natural circumstances. These warriors must be able to discern the supernatural purposes of the natural manifestation. If they are unable to do this, they are in danger of missing the visitation of the Lord on their lives. What's behind me is still in front of some that will read this book. If that is you, I thought you might like some ideas about what I've learned about how to make it through the crossroads, when circumstances you did not imagine, create, invite, or expect - change the direction of your life forever.

Before I list the things that I learned, I think it is important to say that as far as I know, I've never had an original thought. If there is any wisdom in what I will write here, it is because I am a collector of fragments and lessons from other people's spiritual journeys upon which I have built my own. If I could remember where I heard or read certain truths or from whom, I would give the proper attribution. Unfortunately, I cannot remember every person or circumstance or medium where wisdom has been imparted to me. Out of the many words of wisdom and advice that I received during this decade of my life, these are the ones that I have tested and proven to be true.

I once read in a tract from a Michael Marsh meeting that if you want something you have never had, then you must do something you have never done. Or as John Maxwell says it, "If you keep on doing what you've always done, you'll always get what you've always had." It is so very true. My favorite definition of insanity is "doing the same thing over and over and expecting a different result." And yet that is precisely what most of us do. It is because the behavioral patterns that we consider to be comfortable and secure can sometime become strongholds so that we are unable to do anything else. Most of already have what we really want. We may desire other things, but that is not nearly enough to bring about change. A casual desire for something different won't get it for you. You must work for it passionately in circumstances that are sometimes downright unpleasant. But if you will commit your ways unto the Lord, He will light your path. You, however, must move your feet.

I have learned that there is a difference between "trusting" the Lord, and "tempting" the Lord. The Lord has obligated Himself to respond to our faithful attempts to follow Him. He has not, however, obligated Himself to intervene when we, touting our faith as the reason, willfully defy the laws of common sense or cause and effect that He has established as parameters; and then expect Him to rescue us from our own foolish behavior. If we insist on jumping off a 10-story building in defiance of the law of gravity, then we best have packed our own chute. Even Jesus did not attempt His Father in that fashion.

*Luke 4:9 The devil led him to Jerusalem and had him stand on the highest point of the temple. "If you are the Son of God," he said, "throw yourself down from here.*
*Luke 4:10 For it is written: "'He will command his angels concerning you to guard you carefully;*
*Luke 4:11 they will lift you up in their hands, so that you will not strike your foot against a stone.'"*
*Luke 4:12 Jesus answered, "It says: 'Do not put the Lord your God to the test.'"*

We are utterly out of bounds if we think that calling ourselves Christian exempts us from the consequences of foolishness, laziness, or sloth. I have added a personal 11$^{th}$ and 12$^{th}$ commandment to my view of life: (11) Thou shalt not kid thyself. The Lord is not obligated to save us from the battles He has not called us to fight. (12) All things come to her who waits, if she worketh like hell while she waits. All personal prophecy is conditional. What the Lord desires for our lives will not come about only because He desires it. When He speaks over our lives, it is up to us to begin to take the steps to make ready the way of the Lord in our destiny. We can thwart what He has planned for us if we refuse to do the hard work that always accompanies the call.

I've also learned that "Life happens" if you're a Christian and it happens if you are not. I am forever fascinated when Christians attribute

176

every tough break in life to spiritual attack. Sometimes it is, but most of the time it is not. Unfortunately, most of us live lives that are of very little interest to spiritual forces. The bad things that happen to us happen because this is a fallen world and in a fallen world, as the Rabbi said, bad things sometimes happen to good people. But likely as not, many if not most of the bad things that happen to us are the natural consequences of our own decisions. So when something that we did not see coming, rocks the very foundation of our lives, then we better have our lives anchored to something that does not move. We do not get to choose the storms we encounter in life. We do not get to choose our disappointments, our illnesses, our losses. I have come to believe that if we live long enough, each of us will come face to face with the thing we dread the most. And when the storm comes, if we would avoid being crushed against the rocks of circumstances we cannot control, then we must be anchored to something upon which the storms have no effect.

No matter how desperate your circumstance may become, work as if everything depended on you and then close your door and pray as if it depended on God. When "Life happens" to you, you will come to the point where you are so stressed and depressed that you would rather die than face the next day. Before you get there, let me tell you now how to pray to save your life. I had this prayer taped to the corner of my desk for 7 years at channel 23. And when I reached that point of despondency, I read it out loud to the filing cabinet. I knew that the filing cabinet didn't care, but I was announcing where I stood to the spiritual world that whirled about me. I said, "I know how bad things look, but this is how things are. My help comes from the maker of Heaven and Earth. He will not let my foot move and He does not sleep. He keeps me from evil and guards my life. His loving kindness is ever upon me and his love for me is from everlasting to everlasting."

Stand on and up for what you really believe to be true. As a wise person has said, "Stand for something or you will fall for anything." Decide what you believe about God and then believe it with all of your heart and all of your mind. Where is the line for you? What will you die for? Martin Luther King once said, "The person who has nothing worth dying for also has nothing worth living for." When "Life happens," it brings with it circumstances and choices that will put a price tag on what you say you believe. Only you can decide if you will pay it.

When "Life happens", you can survive personal and professional humiliation. You will not like it, but you can survive it. No great victory was ever won without blood, sweat, and tears. When your feet hurt and your head aches and the circumstances are overwhelming, remember what Churchill told the British at the darkest hour of the war: "Never give up. Never, never, never, never, never give up." And when you think you cannot go on, you can. You can if you are a follower of Jesus. Because the same spirit that raised Jesus from the dead is the spirit that is within you.

Understand the truth about fear. One of those clichés that Christians often use is that *fear* is the opposite of *faith*. No, it is not. In fact, *fear* is one of the strongest manifestations of *faith*. The problem is that *fear* is *faith* in your enemy. Fear is the belief that those circumstances, which have come against you, can indeed destroy you. Since you were a child, you have likely been told to stand and face your fear because if you run away, you never stop running.  Standing will work in that you can hold the ground you have, but you don't really make any progress by standing.   I have a much better and far more effective suggestion for you when you come face to face with the thing you fear the most.  I learned it from Pastor Alan Langstaff.

In a pride of lions, when the old lion is too weak to fight anymore he isn't driven from the pride; he is merely given a new job.  He can no longer fight, but he can still roar.  So when the lions hunt and they come upon a prey, perhaps a herd of antelope in a clearing, the old lion will go around to the other side and hide in the weeds and roar.  The antelope hear it, panic, and turn and run *away from the roar*, straight into the jaws of the waiting younger lions.  So this is my final suggestion for you.   When Life happens to you, remember that Christians are notorious for giving up five minutes too soon.  When the Lord calls you to leave the path you know to follow Him in high adventure, you will surely hear the roar of the enemy who stalks about seeking whom he may devour.  If you are a follower of Jesus, do not run away.  That lion is toothless.  And don't just stand there. Take the ground that the Lord is calling you to conquer.  Run *towards* the roar.

# Chapter 10

## Whose Fool Are You?

In chapter one, I made reference to the person who is "somewhat Christian." I feel compelled to write one more chapter of this book for the person who knows that he or she might be described with those words. It is for the person who is saved. Or the person who thinks he is. Somewhere along the way in American Christianity, we developed the strange idea that the salvation that Jesus died for was to keep us out of hell. Nothing more. Once we are satisfied that we have a get-out-of-Hell-free card, we tuck it into our back pocket in case we ever need it and proceed to live our lives in largely the same way we did before we "trusted Christ." A concept, by the way, which has no basis in anything Jesus ever said. Jesus did not say, "Trust me." He said, repent, believe, and follow.

Once along the way, someone asked me if the journey had been harder because I was a woman or because I was a Christian. He was surprised when I said that it was harder being a woman. Why? Because if you are a woman, you cannot hide it. If you are a woman and you are cast into circumstances where someone is biased against women, you need not do anything wrong to meet resistance. All you have to do is show up. But if you are cast into circumstances where someone is biased against Christians, you can sometimes hide that if your faith is inconvenient. It is my observation that more and more people are doing exactly that. We have become a church of the "somewhat Christian." Yes, we believe in Jesus.

We do not, however, believe that Jesus should get out of His church box and have anything whatsoever to do with the "real world." We are very content to have Jesus in the role of "savior." Few are willing to have Him in the role of "Lord." The question is why is that true? And why has "Christian" become a label that so many disdain to have?

There was a time in our nation's history when it was different. There was a time when every resume declared whether or not a person was a member of a church or a synagogue. There was a time when our entire social fabric was held together by a contract of behavior based upon Biblical morality. That is not to say that everyone was a Christian or Jewish, or indeed, that everyone was religious. It was to say, however, that Christian or not, Jewish or not, religious or not, everyone agreed that a society which was built and held together by the high ideals of Biblical morality was a pretty good idea upon which to build a nation. Ideals like "Thou shalt not steal;" "Love your neighbor as yourself;" "Honor your Father and Mother;" "Thou shalt not kill" and the other commandments and teachings of the Bible, were thought to be excellent building blocks for a democracy.

There was a time when this nation was mostly comprised of people of the Jewish faith, Christians and non-Christians. Christians and non-Christians, contrary to what some may think, have co-existed since Constantine declared that Christianity would be the religion of the Roman Empire. Yes there were the Crusades and the Inquisition. But these were wars and persecutions between religions, not wars between Christians and those who are without religious identity. All

Christians know and love someone who is a non-Christian. Christians have no plans to persecute non-Christians as revenge for 1$^{st}$ century atrocities. They love them, pray for them, and try to persuade them to consider the possibility that Jesus really is who He claimed to be. Non-Christians whom I have known or observed are rarely vehemently opposed to Christians. They are simply uninformed as to who Christians are and why. Many times, they simply do not know any Christians. They get their information about what Christians must be like from the popular media. Governor Jesse Ventura of Minnesota walked into a firestorm when he commented that people who went to church were weak-minded and needed a crutch. That idea did not originate with Governor Ventura. So where did it come from?

Most of what any person in America knows about any other person, who does not live next door to them, is known as a result of the consumption of media. For example, I have strong opinions about President Clinton. I have never met President Clinton. I have never engaged in a personal exchange of any sort with him. Yet, I am quite positive that if he walked into my living room, I would know exactly who he was. Why? Because I am familiar with him as he is portrayed in the media. Non-Christians only know Christians as a result of how they are portrayed in the media. And how is that? We rarely make the news unless the lunatic fringe, which is decidedly unchristian and foreign to any doctrine associated with the Christian faith, bombs an abortion clinic. In the entertainment media, the clergy are portrayed as weak or fallen priests in horror movies and salacious love stories. Christian people are often depicted as comic relief in raucous situation comedies. If there is a serious treatment of Christians, it nearly always has to do with someone who is both hypocritical and self-serving, or as someone who is slightly off balance. Michael Medved, a Jewish writer and film critic, wrote an excellent book called <u>Hollywood Vs. America,</u> which addresses the depth and breadth of this problem. If you were a non-Christian and all you knew about the Christian faith was how you saw it portrayed in popular media, which of those images would you aspire to be like? Christians may seem strange to unbelievers, but they are generally considered by them to be relatively harmless.

In the past decade, however, a third group has come to the party. These are the anti-Christians. These people are not uninformed about the claims of the Christian faith. They are people who have made a conscientious decision to reject Jesus Christ and all that is associated with Him. Anti-Christians believe that Christians are not only wrong in their beliefs, but that they are dangerous. Far too often, the mainstream media reinforce this belief by the verbiage they choose in describing the news of the day where Christians or Christian beliefs have surfaced in an issue. For example, in political news, one rarely hears about the religious beliefs of a candidate unless that candidate happens to be a Christian. One of the very sad legacies of the political circus of the past decade is that, in the mind of many Americans, it is less a liability to be an adulterer than it is to be a Christian.

As a result, largely in an attempt to avoid the wrath of the anti-Christians and the media, the fastest growing group in the American church today are those who are "somewhat Christian." These are people who are Christian in name only, with little to no understanding of the tenets of the faith they claim to have. Many of them are in the faith at all as a result of having been sold an idea of cheap grace that cannot be found in any traditional Biblical teaching. The idea of self-sacrifice or of leading a life of discipleship, no matter what profession one may be in, is a foreign and distasteful concept.

The "somewhat Christian" believe that they are saved because they have believed the idea that all a person need do is to say the sinner's prayer and he is immediately guaranteed eternal life no matter what his life looks like after "trusting Christ." If our ideas about salvation and eternal life are based upon what we read in scripture, someone show me where it says that. Here is what my Bible has to say on the subject.

*2 Cor 5:17 Therefore, if anyone is in Christ, he is a new creation; the old has gone, the new has come!*

*Mat 16:24 Then Jesus said to his disciples, "If anyone would come after me, he must deny himself and take up his cross and follow me.*

*John 12:26 Whoever serves me must follow me; and where I am, my servant also will be. My Father will honor the one who serves me.*

*Heb 10:26 If we deliberately keep on sinning after we have received the knowledge of the truth, no sacrifice for sins is left,*
*Heb 10:27 but only a fearful expectation of judgment and of raging fire that will consume the enemies of God.*

*Heb 10:29 How much more severely do you think a man deserves to be punished who has trampled the Son of God under foot, who has treated as an unholy thing the blood of the covenant that sanctified him, and who has insulted the Spirit of grace?*

*Heb 10:36 You need to persevere so that when you have done the will of God, you will receive what he has promised.*

*Heb 3:14 We have come to share in Christ if we hold firmly till the end the confidence we had at first.*

Let me be clear. Salvation comes by grace through faith as a gift from God. It is free and unearned by man. But we are on dangerous ground if we play word games with so precious a gift.

*Gal 6:7 Do not be deceived: God cannot be mocked. A man reaps what he sows.*

*Gal 6:8 The one who sows to please his sinful nature, from that nature will reap destruction; the one who sows to please the Spirit, from the Spirit will reap eternal life.*

*Gal 6:9 Let us not become weary in doing good, for at the proper time we will reap a harvest if we do not give up.*

What does it mean to have the kind of faith through which God's unmerited grace provides salvation? It does not mean saying a few sentences to flatter Jesus. Saving faith has little or nothing to do with what we *say* we believe. In America, we say things we don't really mean as a matter of course. Words have become cheap. What we say we "have faith in" and what we say we "believe in" is only true when manifested in one way: through what we do. If we want to know what a person truly believes, look at what he does. God will not be mocked. We are on a very slippery slope if we continue to entice sinners into the redemption of Jesus Christ without telling them that the witness of salvation is a changed life. A person who has the faith in Jesus that brings salvation will not continue to live a life of deliberate and continual sin. If he does, someone needs to ask him the question. How saved are you? Jesus died so that we could be free from our sin. Repentance means that we agree with Jesus about the nature of sin. Because we agree, we turn and go a different way from where we were before. He did not die so that we could be comfortable in continuing in the same sin He came to free us from.

Life will happen to the "somewhat Christian" just as it happens to everyone else. The "somewhat Christian" will also arrive at the crossroads of his life. The day will come when circumstances that he did not expect will place a price tag on the faith he claims to have. His faith will be tested and shown for what it is. Life at the crossroads will be different for the true follower of Jesus Christ and the "somewhat Christian" because of the Word each has received. If the Word he received landed in soil that had not been properly prepared, he will not be able to stand against the onslaught of the enemy. Because of the circumstances that have come against him, he will deny the faith that he hoped would save him

*Mat 13:3   Then he told them many things in parables, saying: "A farmer went out to sow his seed.*

*Mat 13:4 As he was scattering the seed, some fell along the path, and the birds came and ate it up.*
*Mat 13:5 Some fell on rocky places, where it did not have much soil. It sprang up quickly, because the soil was shallow.*
*Mat 13:6 But when the sun came up, the plants were scorched, and they withered because they had no root.*

When the same storm comes to the Christian who is a follower of Jesus, the Christian will stand.

*Mat 13:8 Still other seed fell on good soil, where it produced a crop--a hundred, sixty or thirty times what was sown.*

The "somewhat Christian" will not stand because he cannot stand. He has been caught unaware. He has not been trained in spiritual warfare. Not only does he not know what his Bible says about his circumstances; he does not know where his Bible is.

The church must realize that the "somewhat Christian" is what we are turning out by the thousands, if not tens of thousands, as a result of what passes for Christian teaching today. If it were not true, then the church would not be losing adherents faster than any other institution in America, as reported in Barna's The Second Coming of the Church. Barna goes on to say that the adult believer who "comes to Jesus" today is no longer affiliated with any church after just 6 weeks of his so called conversion. Further, if this were not true, then our culture would not be in the free fall that it is in.

Dr. David Noble, Executive Director and Founder of Summit Ministries in Colorado Springs, speaks frequently at Worldview Weekends on the state of Christianity in American colleges and universities. Dr. Noble refers to a startling statistic. He declares that 50% of the evangelical kids coming out of Christian households today, and who attend a secular university, will renounce their Christian beliefs within two years of entering the university. If that is true, whose fault is it?

Let's consider another scenario. Suppose that we received statistical data that demonstrated that 50% of the kids who came out of public schools would flunk out of college by the end of their sophomore year. We would be outraged. We would want answers. Whose fault is it? Without doubt, all eyes would turn to the pubic school system. Whose fault is it if we are losing our church raised kids to secular thought in only 2 years of college? At some point, we have to be honest and say that there is something very wrong with what we are teaching them in the church about what faith in Jesus Christ is really all about.

At the end of the day, the church consists only of the men and women who are in it. It is the laity who makes up the church, not the professional clergy. It is the job of the pastors, preachers, teachers and apostles to equip and make ready the royal priesthood of believers so that they understand who they are in the kingdom of God and are prepared to participate in the great spiritual battle that is still before us. It is crucial that we change tactics and make every believer a minister of the church. Why? Because the church is the only force in America that is challenging Satan's claim to an entire generation. The "somewhat Christian" will not win the battle.

In the beginning of this book, I said that this book is intended for eagles, warlords, and kings. If you were not in that category, you would have put this book down long ago. If you are still reading, then you are among the mature and this is a message only for the mature. Those who are babes in the faith cannot process these last pages. We must come to understand that we cannot be true followers, disciples, friends of Jesus and be "somewhat Christian" at the same time. We cannot agree with Jesus and agree with Satan at the same time. We must decide where we stand. We must *follow* Jesus not just *believe* in Jesus. If He is not Lord *of* all, then He is not Lord *at* all.

*James 2:19  You believe that there is one God. Good! Even the demons believe that--and shudder. James 2:20  You foolish man, do you want evidence that faith without deeds is useless?*

Once begun, we must continue on the journey. We win no crowns for starting the race, only for finishing the race. We must be prepared. As Jim Elliot said, we must be ready to "lose the things we cannot keep, to keep the things we cannot lose." The devil is much more clever than we give him credit for. You will not see him coming until he meets you at the crossroads of your life. And he will meet you there with the thing you fear or value the most. You must be ready when you get there.

Long before I ever heard of Gannett, I had already made the most important decision of my life. That I would believe in and follow Jesus as the Holy Spirit enabled me. I could never do it in my own strength. But as the Comforter helped me, I would not be ashamed of the gospel of Jesus Christ no matter who, no matter what. When I left KARE in humiliation it was the hardest moment of my life. I had always been a person whom other people had respected and followed. Now I was a person who was laughed at, pitied by my friends, and thought a fool by the same people whose respect I once had. The week I left, one of the tabloids said that my career was a tragedy and that I was typical of those who abandoned common sense for the privilege of being "fools for Jesus." Perhaps the tabloids were right. It is very possible that I was precisely that: a fool for Jesus.

So I end this book with a bit of advice and a question for those kings among you who are on your way to your personal crossroads. Make up your mind before you get there. Don't wait until the crisis to determine where you stand with Jesus. If you wait until the crisis, you will not make a good decision. Choose whom you will serve. Because if you are not a fool for Jesus, then whose fool are you?